Large Print

CROSSWORD PUZZLES FOR EVERYONE

100 CROSSWORDS

Copyright © 2021 by Mary Widkins. All rights Reserved.

No part of this publication or the information in it may be quoted from or reproduced in any form by means such as printing, scanning, photocopying or otherwise without prior written permission of the copyright holder.

Disclaimer and Terms of Use: Effort has been made to ensure that the information in this book is accurate and complete, however, the author and the publisher do not warrant the accuracy of the information, text and graphics contained within the book due to the rapidly changing nature of science, research, known and unknown facts and the Internet. The Author and the publisher do not hold any responsibility for errors, omissions or contrary interpretation of the subject matter herein.

Crossword
PUZZLES

In your hands a super-collection for smart leisure - classic crosswords.

And most importantly, all the task are original, many forms of puzzles were invented by the author and published for the first time in this book.

Choose any task to your taste and practice erudition!

All you need for this is a pencil, a little free time and intellectual excitement!

puzzle 3

ACROSS
1. Neuter singular pronoun
3. Gem
7. Quarantine
9. Prefix meaning not
11. Middle Eastern bread
12. Yoko -
13. Prefix meaning without
15. Perform
16. Part of a circle
17. Jack in cribbage
19. Pal
21. Enough
23. Name
24. Land measure
25. Objective case of I
27. Therefore
28. Mature
29. Nimbus
31. In the direction of
32. Kidney bean
34. Necessities
35. Prefix meaning without

DOWN
1. Part of the verb to be
2. Apex
3. Jet-assisted takeoff
4. Greek letter
5. Plural of I
6. Soothing medicine
7. Vapid
8. Bottle top
10. Negative vote
12. Toward the mouth
14. Polygon having nine sides
16. Part of the verb "to be"
18. Drill
20. Torpedo vessel (1-4)
22. Plural of I
25. Red planet
26. Biblical high priest
28. Near to
29. Possessed
30. Wood sorrel
32. Masculine pronoun
33. Not off

puzzle 4

ACROSS
1. Prefix meaning not
3. Black wood
7. Psalmbook
9. Not off
11. Restrain
12. To and -
13. Belonging to
15. Plural of I
16. Family
17. Jack in cribbage
19. Give food to
21. Prefix, thousand
23. Go wrong
24. Garbage can
25. To exist
27. Therefore
28. Peak
29. Ego
31. Objective case of I
32. Flatfish
34. Stalks
35. Part of the verb to be

DOWN
1. Part of the verb to be
2. Arrest
3. Suffix, diminutive
4. Hive insect
5. Otherwise
6. Types of cricket deliveries
7. Fall heavily
8. Statute
10. Negative vote
12. Run from
14. Weaknesses
16. Providing
18. Radar screen element
20. Legal right
22. Not off
25. Units of loudness
26. Biblical high priest
28. Part of the verb "to be"
29. Uncle -, USA personified
30. Law enforcement agency
32. Masculine pronoun
33. Objective case of we

puzzle 5

ACROSS
1. Toward the top
3. Hipbone
7. Sleeping sickness flies
9. Prefix meaning not
11. Whimper
12. Fuss
13. Depart
15. To exist
16. Prefix, foot
17. Raises
19. Angered
21. Seasoning
23. Yoko -
24. Dove's call
25. Similar to
27. Therefore
28. Coxa
29. Bucket
31. Neuter singular pronoun
32. Hindu religious retreats
34. Abominable snowmen
35. Plural of I

DOWN
1. Objective case of we
2. Energy
3. Small island
4. Sheltered side
5. Part of the verb to be
6. Refuse heaps
7. Spanish river
8. Vat
10. Negative vote
12. Prefix, air
14. The state of being opaque
16. The ratio between circumference and diameter
18. Splash
20. Ill-fates
22. In the direction of
25. Exclamations of surprise
26. Knight's title
28. Hello there
29. Pressure symbol
30. Statute
32. Near to
33. Objective case of I

puzzle 6

ACROSS
1. Cooking implement
4. Emperor of Russia
8. My, French (Plural)
11. Level
13. Jumble
14. Family
15. Risque
16. Mean
18. Tearful
20. Sound
21. Foreign
23. Long-leaved lettuce
24. Sea eagle
25. Indian pulses
27. Wanes
31. Reclined
33. Highest mountain in Crete
34. Swing around
35. Stable attendant
36. Be defeated
38. Play division
39. Shoemaker's tool
41. Piles
43. Cavalry sword
46. Hit
47. Roman capital of Palestine
49. Clump of trees
52. Land measure
53. Tidy
54. Wallaroo
55. Scottish hill
56. Withered
57. Bind

DOWN
1. Each
2. Eggs
3. Constructive
4. British statesman
5. Whimsically comical
6. Question
7. Prefix, nose
8. Skirt coming to just below knee
9. Old cloth measures
10. Inner Hebrides island
12. Russian no
17. Nuzzles
19. Assist
21. Long fish
22. Photograph of bones (1-3)
23. School class member
26. Fuss
28. Total cut off of all light
29. Male of the deer
30. Hardens
32. Draws close to
37. Greek letter
40. Trains away from
42. Pinnacle
43. Strike breaker
44. River in central Switzerland
45. "Has - ". Person who once was
46. Scorch
48. Female ruff
50. Prefix, three
51. Pedal digit

puzzle 7

ACROSS
1. Mouth part
4. Sprint contest
8. Raincoat
11. Son of Isaac and Rebekah
13. Dash
14. Primate
15. Paddles
16. Person who gardens
18. Sponsorship
20. Avoid
21. Hollow-nosed bullet
23. Carp-like fish
24. The self
25. Honey liquor
27. U.S. space agency
31. 12th month of the Jewish calendar
33. Not
34. Catch
35. Funeral fire
36. Norse god of thunder
38. Island (France)
39. Printer's measures
41. Spectres
43. Cavalry sword
46. Investigation
47. Roman capital of Palestine
49. Cause of scratching
52. Land measure
53. Lowest high tide
54. Sewing case
55. Scottish hill
56. Third son of Adam
57. Bitter vetch

DOWN
1. Zodiac sign
2. Mount - , N.W. Qld. mining town
3. Illicit lover
4. Military groups
5. Woe is me
6. Automobile
7. Finished
8. Supernatural power
9. Mimicked
10. Wax
12. Second-hand
17. Equalises
19. Common eucalypt
21. Profound
22. Unattractive
23. Ideogram
26. Exclamation of surprise
28. Aniseed liqueur
29. Seasoning
30. Matures
32. Ogles
37. 17th letter of the Greek alphabet
40. Income
42. Off-Broadway theater award
43. Strike breaker
44. River in central Switzerland
45. "Has - ". Person who once was
46. Bog fuel
48. Female ruff
50. Worthless dog
51. Belonging to him

puzzle 8

ACROSS
1. Letter Z
4. Stand
8. The sun
11. Food scraps
13. Wanes
14. Top card
15. Double curve
16. Sweet courses
18. The base of a number system
20. Farewell
21. Small sandpiper
23. Optic organ
24. Prefix, over
25. Ova
27. Flaky mineral
31. Snug
33. Breakfast cereal
34. Once again
35. Leg joint
36. Type of jazz
38. Beer
39. - kwon do (Korean martial art)
41. Animals
43. Garden pest
46. Photograph book
47. State of USA
49. Regretted
52. Expression of disgust
53. Employs
54. Pinnacle
55. Your
56. Sprint
57. Colour

DOWN
1. Menagerie
2. Work unit
3. Perpetuate
4. Double-breasted overcoat
5. Mountain goat
6. Ethnic telecaster
7. Short story
8. Hindu garment
9. Prefix, eight
10. Minus
12. Marine mammal
17. Dropsy
19. Expire
21. Ship's floor
22. On top of
23. Set up
26. Needlefish
28. In view of the fact
29. Gael
30. Inspires dread
32. Abominable snowmen
37. Debutante
40. Audibly
42. Subtle emanation
43. Filth
44. Near
45. Wan
46. Greek god of war
48. America (Abbr)
50. Australian bird
51. Scottish river

puzzle 9

ACROSS
1. Go wrong
4. Tiller
8. Prefix, three
11. Indian nursemaid
13. Double curve
14. A dynasty in China
15. Indian queen
16. Nonchalant (4-4)
18. Burn with water
20. Zodiac sign
21. Feebly
23. Biblical high priest
24. Part of a circle
25. Female sheep
27. Wanes
31. Prefer
33. Breakfast cereal
34. Worry
35. Trial
36. Auricular
38. Yoko -
39. Possessed
41. Ancient fortress in Israel
43. Suffix, city
46. Loaded cargo
47. Squarely
49. Absent
52. Cyst envelope
53. Nobleman
54. Molten rock
55. Attempt
56. Levee
57. Yes

DOWN
1. Otic organ
2. Handwoven Scandinavian rug
3. Pillages
4. Tinseltown
5. Minor oath
6. Garland
7. Award of honour
8. Siamese
9. Sprint contest
10. Writing fluids
12. Rube
17. Short
19. Beer
21. - Disney
22. A Great Lake
23. Able to be estimated
26. Consume
28. Major avenue in New York City
29. Curve
30. Portico
32. Moral code
37. Bounder
40. Inquired
42. Marine mammal
43. Surreptitious, attention getting sound
44. - Khayyam
45. Lacelike
46. Songbird
48. Time of sunshine
50. Greeting
51. Yelp

puzzle 10

ACROSS
1. Talent
4. Gaiter
8. Girl (Slang)
11. Hawaiian honeycreeper
13. Australian super-model
14. Top card
15. Drudge
16. Disappointments (3-5)
18. Athlete's foot
20. Fools
21. Red dye
23. Island of Denmark
24. Cheer
25. Bicycle
27. A bloke
31. Once again
33. Rocky peak
34. Wallaroo
35. Serving plate
36. Food
38. Sea (French)
39. Observation
41. Inhabitant of Ionia
43. Growl
46. Pasted
47. Seaport in S Sardinia
49. Notch
52. Prefix, one
53. Seaport in NE Egypt
54. Sewing case
55. Level of karate proficiency
56. Inner Hebrides island
57. Japanese currency

DOWN
1. Intention
2. - de Janeiro
3. Quick, jerky movements
4. Mythical moon-dwellers
5. Prayer
6. High-pitched
7. Woman's one-piece undergarment
8. Gape
9. Adolescent pimples
10. Minus
12. Tennis star, - Natase
17. Weight measure
19. Pen point
21. Toward the mouth
22. Indian queen
23. Enrich
26. Hawaiian acacia
28. Dampness
29. Region
30. Pornography (Colloq)
32. Verticil
37. Former coin of France
40. Ecstasy
42. Hawaiian goose
43. Driving shower
44. Grandmother
45. Against
46. Hoar
48. Diving bird
50. Prompt
51. Relation

puzzle 11

ACROSS
1. Nautical, rear
4. Worry
8. Marry
11. Ark builder
13. First class (1-3)
14. An age
15. Prefix, ten
16. Skin preparation
18. Covered with ivy
20. Wood smoothing tool
21. Notice
23. Dined
24. Atomic mass unit
25. Ireland
27. Growl
31. Italian currency
33. Paddle
34. American university
35. Sea eagle
36. On top of
38. Prefix, not
39. Vapour
41. Tilted
43. Suffix, city
46. Dizzy
47. Extremely successful play or record (5-3)
49. Old
52. Cyst envelope
53. Relax
54. Man
55. Attempt
56. Drunkards
57. Island (France)

DOWN
1. Also
2. Enemy
3. Not inclined to conversation
4. Humorous
5. Crucifix
6. Abstract being
7. Seduce
8. Scorpion-like N.Z. insect
9. Ireland
10. Fresh-water fish
12. Possess
17. Funeral oration
19. Freeze
21. Valley
22. Islamic chieftain
23. Meteors
26. Knock with knuckles
28. Redfish
29. Agave
30. Tear
32. Sponsorship
37. - Kelly
40. Australia vs England cricket trophy
42. First man
43. Surreptitious, attention getting sound
44. - Khayyam
45. Lacelike
46. Pith
48. Monetary unit of Vietnam
50. Former measure of length
51. Scottish river

puzzle 12

ACROSS
1. Prefix, one
4. Church recess
8. Excavate
11. Relax
13. Lighting gas
14. Revised form of Esperanto
15. Shout
16. Valuer
18. A poplar
20. Twinned crystal
21. Small dark-purple plum
23. Morose
24. Israeli submachine gun
25. Show disgust or strong dislike
27. Metal band
31. Nap
33. Take to court
34. Official language of Pakistan
35. Level
36. Lazy
38. Corded fabric
39. - and don'ts
41. Diners
43. Modernise
46. Fragrant oil
47. Companion of Daniel
49. Mature
52. Decay
53. Ireland
54. Golf mounds
55. Abstract being
56. Levels of karate proficiency
57. Vital tree fluid

DOWN
1. U-turn (Colloq)
2. Not
3. Convert to Islam
4. Reminiscence
5. Mexican currency
6. Distress signal
7. Purgative injection
8. Circular plate
9. Object of worship
10. Pierce with horn
12. Old cloth measures
17. Hindu ascetic
19. Very good (1-2)
21. City-dweller holidaying on a ranch
22. Northern arm of the Black Sea
23. Bones
26. Rumen
28. Planetariums
29. River in central Europe
30. Young dogs
32. Finished
37. Consume
40. Possessed
42. Pastry item
43. Uncommon
44. Black
45. Devices for fishing
46. Against
48. An age
50. Legume
51. Extrasensory perception

puzzle 13

ACROSS
1. - Mahal
4. Capital of Yemen
8. That woman
11. Auricular
13. Wax
14. A month
15. Demonstration
16. Wheel
18. Fooled
20. Strictness
21. Stirrup
23. Hallucinogenic drug
24. Grain beard
25. At sea
27. Sea eagle
31. Repeat
33. Family
34. Marsh plant
35. Unlocking implements
36. Town crier's call
38. To silence
39. Tavern
41. Resembling a foot
43. Television
46. Iodine solution
47. Make sour
49. Ireland
52. Beak
53. Redact
54. Stalk
55. Superlative suffix
56. Profit failure
57. Affirmative response

DOWN
1. Fox
2. Dined
3. Superior quality
4. Something added
5. Deceased
6. Go wrong
7. Draws close to
8. Polluted atmosphere
9. Nimbus
10. Looker
12. Masterstroke
17. Apple drink
19. Legume
21. Shirt
22. Affectedly dainty
23. Wordsworth, Coleridge, and Southey (4.5)
26. Cathedral city
28. Sovereignty
29. Tidy
30. Brink
32. Willow
37. Last letter
40. Prize named after inventor of dynamite
42. Performs
43. Weathercock
44. Frozen confections
45. Something owing
46. Inflammation (Suffix)
48. Fuss
50. Female ruff
51. Printer's measures

puzzle 14

ACROSS
1. Great gladness
4. Complacent
8. Brown-capped boletus mushroom
11. Dutch cheese
13. River in central Switzerland
14. In the past
15. Diminish
16. Selenographer
18. Language spoken in S China
20. Tears
21. Unlocked
23. Avail of
24. Female ruff
25. Paradise
27. Indian pulses
31. 27th president of the U.S
33. Affirmative vote
34. Foot part
35. Inner Hebrides island
36. Yes
38. Actor, - Chaney
39. Purulence
41. Disencumbered
43. Foreign
46. Place
47. Along with this
49. Routine
52. Eggs
53. 12th month of the Jewish calendar
54. It was
55. - and Yang
56. Refuse
57. Hard-shelled fruit

DOWN
1. Semite
2. Room within a harem
3. Cause to acquire Yankee traits
4. Period of youthful inexperience
5. Island in central Hawaii
6. Vase
7. Cogs
8. First son of Adam and Eve
9. Minor oath
10. Part of the brainstem
12. Intend
17. Marsh plants
19. Scottish river
21. Food scraps
22. Alp
23. Ghostly
26. Optic organ
28. Limitation
29. Agave
30. Advance money
32. Wigwam
37. Hasten
40. Unmarried
42. Blow-pipe missile
43. Nautical call
44. Son of Jacob and Leah
45. Republic in SW Asia
46. Daze
48. Island (France)
50. Greek letter
51. Superlative suffix

puzzle 15

ACROSS
1. Greek letter
4. Barge
8. Actress, - West
11. Ethereal
13. A Great Lake
14. Sicken
15. Harp-like instrument
16. Region of calm winds
18. Pertaining to the ileum
20. Semblance
21. Small nut
23. Japanese currency
24. America (Abbr)
25. Italian currency
27. Egyptian goddess of fertility
31. Measure out
33. Large tub
34. Pointed end
35. Make beer
36. Nestling
38. Island (France)
39. Printer's measures
41. Blew intermittently
43. Aggression (Colloq)
46. Greek letter
47. A great dispersion of a common people
49. Capable
52. Sick
53. Dash
54. Jelly-like mass
55. - kwon do (Korean martial art)
56. Clarets
57. Teenage lout

DOWN
1. Mate
2. Attention-getting call
3. Pique
4. Tranquillisers
5. Crocodile (Colloq)
6. Lubricant
7. Chock
8. Island in central Hawaii
9. Intentions
10. Otherwise
12. Shout
17. Mysterious
19. Conger
21. Unfeeling
22. Consumer
23. Turkish swords
26. Sunbeam
28. Featly
29. Small island
30. Raced
32. Pitchers
37. Take to court
40. Sulky person
42. Pierce with knife
43. Entrance
44. Venomous lizard
45. Strong wind
46. Type of jazz
48. Bullfight call
50. Card game
51. Wane

puzzle 16

ACROSS
1. Questioning exclamation
4. Was indebted
8. Sphere
11. Enough
13. Alter
14. Court
15. Staple Oriental grain
16. Nervousness
18. New Zealand evergreen tree
20. Knobs
21. Church walkways
23. Russian secret police
24. Scale note
25. Argument
27. 12th month of the Jewish calendar
31. Small particle
33. Information
34. Floor covering
35. Father
36. Detest
38. Russian plane
39. To date
41. Merriment
43. Situated on an axis
46. Rekindled
47. Having parts deleted for moral purposes
49. South African river
52. Abstract being
53. Sharp pain
54. Jason's ship
55. Drunkard
56. Suffix, diminutive
57. Japanese currency

DOWN
1. That woman
2. Prefix, one
3. Pawnshop
4. Careless omission
5. Dry riverbed
6. Work unit
7. Expiring
8. Was indebted
9. Fragrant flower
10. Employer
12. Welt
17. Prize named after inventor of dynamite
19. U-turn (Colloq)
21. As soon as possible
22. Jot
23. Scrap metal used as ballast
26. New Zealand parrot
28. Serving as a limit
29. Military detachment
30. Lethargic
32. Yucatan indians
37. Conger
40. Run off
42. Exclamation of acclaim
43. Beats by tennis service
44. Prefix, foreign
45. Current month
46. Hire
48. Rodent
50. Mature
51. Actor, - Chaney

puzzle 17

ACROSS
1. Norse goddess
4. Arab vessel
8. Question
11. Large African antelope
13. Take by force
14. Grandmother
15. Belly
16. Resembling a goose
18. Prudes
20. Edible red seaweed
21. Education facility
23. Egyptian serpent
24. Monetary unit of Vietnam
25. Pleasing
27. Fencing sword
31. Inflammation (Suffix)
33. And not
34. Ireland
35. Style
36. Redact
38. W.A. river
39. Donkey
41. Church walkways
43. Fissile rock
46. A poplar
47. State of USA
49. Russian secret police
52. Anger
53. Employs
54. South American bird
55. An infusion
56. Final
57. Biblical high priest

DOWN
1. In what way?
2. An age
3. Resembling lymph
4. Large mining excavators
5. - Christian Andersen
6. Operations (colloq)
7. Unwanted plants
8. Indigo
9. Without
10. Leg joint
12. Prefix, dry
17. Indian currency
19. Charged particle
21. Spacing wedge
22. Roman censor
23. Trapeze artist
26. Food fish
28. Preface
29. Ireland
30. Finishes
32. Marine mammals
37. - Maria, coffee liqueur
40. South Korea's capital
42. Polluted atmosphere
43. Struck
44. Rent
45. At sea
46. Greek god of war
48. America (Abbr)
50. Mate
51. Prefix, one

puzzle 18

ACROSS
1. Fish eggs
4. Political combine
8. Top card
11. Arm bone
13. Narrow country road
14. Crow call
15. Network
16. Payment for after hours work
18. Chocolate powder
20. Downy duck
21. Satiated
23. Doctrine
24. Japanese currency
25. Walk wearily
27. Wanes
31. Club-like weapon
33. First woman
34. Bargain event
35. Paradise
36. Beach feature
38. Prompt
39. Operations (colloq)
41. Animal with tusks
43. Manila hemp plant
46. Formed by mixing
47. Having rickets
49. Snug
52. Land measure
53. Chapter of the Koran
54. New Guinea currency unit
55. Cot
56. Jump in figure skating
57. Corded fabric

DOWN
1. Odd
2. Bullfight call
3. Hide securely
4. Without blood
5. Molten rock
6. Monad
7. Roman goddess of agriculture
8. Etching fluid
9. Arrived
10. Pitcher
12. Nautical call
17. Occasions
19. Brown-capped boletus mushroom
21. Type of inflorescence
22. Heavy metal
23. The same
26. Eggs
28. Illicit method
29. Sky colour
30. Prophet
32. Methuselah's father
37. Top pupil
40. Monetary unit of India
42. Cult
43. Semite
44. Naked
45. Beaten by tennis service
46. Bog
48. Tuxedo
50. Letter Z
51. Yelp

puzzle 19

ACROSS
1. An infusion
4. Overacts
8. Mothers
11. Capital of Western Samoa
13. First man
14. Food scrap
15. Lively dances
16. Ideal quality
18. Train tracks
20. Flower part
21. Skilled people
23. Snow runner
24. Protrude
25. Portico
27. Ostrich-like bird
31. Against
33. Nocturnal bird
34. Hamlet
35. Marsh plant
36. Lowest high tide
38. Falsehood
39. Dined
41. Stopped
43. 1st letter of the Greek alphabet
46. Titan
47. Horse with a golden coat
49. Adolescent
52. Greek letter
53. Son of Isaac and Rebekah
54. Ireland
55. Timid
56. Black birds
57. Singer, - "King" Cole

DOWN
1. - Mahal
2. Prefix, over
3. Plume
4. Pellet of hail
5. Appends
6. Actress, - West
7. Hit
8. Drudge
9. Ostentatious
10. River of Hades
12. As soon as possible
17. Scottish lord
19. Sexless things
21. Slightly open
22. Sand hill
23. Lecherous
26. Be indebted
28. Breed of dairy cattle
29. A Great Lake
30. Mimicked
32. State in the NW United States
37. Legume
40. Domesticated
42. Poker stake
43. Primates
44. Slat
45. Stage show
46. Chew on a bone
48. Mount - , N.W. Qld. mining town
50. An age
51. Seine

puzzle 20

ACROSS
1. The (German)
4. Viper's tooth
8. Large tub
11. Egg-shaped
13. Double curve
14. Poem
15. List of dishes
16. Turn into a robot
18. Bright arc light
20. Dandies
21. Monetary unit
23. Jewel
24. Japanese sash
25. Network
27. Object of worship
31. Hog sound
33. Primate
34. Information
35. Prefix, large
36. Roman censor
38. Spasm
39. Expression of disgust
41. Roof with straw
43. Below
46. Adult females
47. Vitamin deficiency disease
49. Peruse
52. Mount - , N.W. Qld. mining town
53. Town crier's call
54. Capital of Norway
55. Pig enclosure
56. Hawaiian goose
57. Ethnic telecaster

DOWN
1. Benedictine monk's title
2. First woman
3. Festering
4. Maintain headway
5. Eager
6. Beak
7. Rock cavity
8. Empty
9. Hoe-shaped axe
10. Golf mounds
12. Soothe
17. Swollen
19. Braggart (Colloq) (1.2)
21. Fate
22. Off-Broadway theater award
23. Segregate in a ghetto
26. Mineral spring
28. Foolishness
29. Auricular
30. Slat
32. New Zealand evergreen tree
37. Electrical resistance unit
40. Republic in W equatorial Africa
42. Prefix, air
43. Sacred Egyptian bird
44. Nidus
45. Ravel
46. Songbird
48. Optic organ
50. Long-sleeved linen vestment
51. - and don'ts

puzzle 21

ACROSS
1. Sly animal
4. Reverberate
8. Wane
11. Republic in SW Asia
13. Uproar
14. Yes
15. Hawaiian goose
16. Mentally transported
18. Forbidden
20. Overjoy
21. Capital of Iran
23. Part of a circle
24. Room within a harem
25. Garment edges
27. Sea eagles
31. Good-bye (2-2)
33. Killer whale
34. Harvest
35. Portent
36. Second-hand
38. Atomic mass unit
39. Vapour
41. Suckler
43. Kingdom
46. Notions
47. Good digestion
49. Deride
52. Land measure
53. Grass around house
54. Matures
55. Very modern
56. Redact
57. Seine

DOWN
1. Fish part
2. Crude mineral
3. Salt of xanthic acid
4. Mistaken
5. Goodbye
6. Jump
7. Marine mammal
8. Jaguarundi
9. Root vegetable
10. Past tense of bid
12. Close to
17. Peptic complaint
19. Expression of contempt
21. In -, in all
22. Dutch cheese
23. An ancestor
26. Missus
28. Reallocate
29. Title
30. Goad
32. Fish
37. Owing
40. Sufficient
42. Hindu music
43. Quantity of paper
44. Wallaroo
45. Mimicked
46. Hawaiian honeycreeper
48. Morose
50. Hive insect
51. Superlative suffix

puzzle 22

ACROSS
1. Henpeck
4. Small valley
8. Poem
11. As previously given
13. Otherwise
14. Bashful
15. Something not to be done (2-2)
16. Real estate register
18. The Hunter
20. Fern seed
21. Disease carrier
23. Meadow
24. Black bird
25. Never
27. Roman censor
31. Ore deposit
33. - Maria, coffee liqueur
34. Black
35. Female sheep
36. U.S. TV award
38. Groove
39. Soil
41. Prefix, liver
43. Swindler
46. Water filled defences
47. Housewife
49. Assistant
52. Noah's vessel
53. 16th letter of the Hebrew alphabet
54. Gardening tools
55. Golf peg
56. Come to ground
57. Seine

DOWN
1. A fool
2. Fuss
3. Racial extermination
4. Adorned
5. Dash
6. Hallucinogenic drug
7. Rent agreement
8. Prefix, eight
9. Performer
10. Australian explorer
12. Three-year-old salmon
17. Room
19. Charged particle
21. Valley
22. Enough
23. Bloodhound
26. Edge
28. Scraped spot or area
29. Solicit
30. Upon
32. S-bends
37. Yes
40. Liver, kidneys or tripe
42. Egyptian deity
43. Steps descending to a river
44. River in central Switzerland
45. Use atomic bom on (Colloq)
46. Chief
48. Handwoven Scandinavian rug
50. Scottish river
51. Superlative suffix

puzzle 23

ACROSS
1. America (Abbr)
4. Hindu sect
8. Diving bird
11. Ilex
13. Notion
14. Pressure symbol
15. Vapour
16. Not a direct hit
18. Indian river
20. Brings up
21. Bounders
23. Gymnasium
24. Expression of disgust
25. Ireland
27. Ornamental brooch
31. Bristle
33. Heavy weight
34. Swing around
35. Unlocking implements
36. Decorated cake
38. Prefix, three
39. It is
41. Fencing sword
43. American witch hunt city
46. American witch hunt city
47. Ball of hair
49. Insane
52. Vase
53. European mountain range
54. Agitate
55. Decade
56. U.S. TV award
57. Etcetera

DOWN
1. Television frequency
2. Former coin of France
3. God
4. Sinus inflammation
5. Roman dates
6. New Zealand parrot
7. Annoy
8. Capital of Western Samoa
9. Former Soviet Union
10. Osculate
12. List of dishes
17. Brief notes
19. Scottish river
21. Teething biscuit
22. Double curve
23. Ordinarily
26. Fabulous bird
28. Eventual
29. Remedy
30. Scion
32. Flower
37. Indian dish
40. Dye
42. Clothesline clips
43. Closed
44. River in central Switzerland
45. Waterfall
46. Close hard
48. Limb
50. British, a fool
51. Part of a circle

puzzle 24

ACROSS
1. Drinking vessel
4. Indian pulses
8. 9th letter of the Hebrew alphabet
11. Second-hand
13. First class (1-3)
14. An age
15. Ursa
16. Woman who is a votary
18. Musk-yielding cat
20. Weathercocks
21. Become more intense
23. Garland
24. Clumsy person
25. Fencing sword
27. Delays
31. Thrash
33. Eggs
34. Shoo
35. Earthen pot
36. Spawning area of salmon
38. Bashful
39. Hard-shelled fruit
41. Likely to change
43. Searches for
46. Lubricated
47. Pursuant
49. Long fish
52. Work unit
53. Curved entrance
54. Break suddenly
55. - and don'ts
56. English court
57. An infusion

DOWN
1. Young bear
2. Avail of
3. Free from strife
4. Type of sofa
5. Loud derisory cry
6. Social insect
7. Depart
8. Adolescent
9. Gaelic
10. Soviet news service
12. Drop moisture
17. Train tracks
19. Victory sign
21. Extinct bird
22. Nobleman
23. Decorative window pane
26. First woman
28. Chance
29. Jail
30. Eye inflammation
32. Financial institutions
37. Indian dish
40. Customary
42. Hive insects
43. Raced
44. Wallaroo
45. Work units
46. At one time
48. Anger
50. New Guinea seaport
51. Mineral spring

puzzle 25

ACROSS
1. Merry
4. Rube
8. Norse goddess
11. Having wings
13. At sea
14. Eggs
15. Mother of Apollo
16. Brave
18. Leaning
20. Old womanish
21. Keyboard instruments
23. Greek letter
24. Exclamation of surprise
25. Pierce with knife
27. Hew
31. Summit of a small hill
33. Exclamation of surprise
34. Ballet skirt
35. Prefix, Chinese
36. Grandmother
38. Rummy game
39. Avail of
41. Introduce
43. Electric discharge
46. Stage whisper
47. Capital of Finland
49. Against
52. Anger
53. Riding strap
54. Howl
55. Victory sign
56. Lengthy
57. - kwon do (Korean martial art)

DOWN
1. Girl (Slang)
2. Beer
3. Turkish sword
4. Pellet of hail
5. Is not
6. Prefix, whale
7. Unit for measuring gold
8. American Indian
9. Sinister
10. Burden
12. Roster
17. Make law
19. - and outs, intricacies
21. Large trees
22. Indian queen
23. Finishing in imitation of ebony
26. Exclamation of surprise
28. French Protestant
29. Auricular
30. Bet
32. Decants
37. Black bird
40. Bagpipe sound
42. June 6, 1944
43. Switchblade
44. Father
45. To the sheltered side
46. Related
48. Prefix, new
50. Two
51. Island (France)

puzzle 26

ACROSS
1. Ointment
5. Frizzy hair style
9. Talent
12. Fencing sword
13. South-east Asian nation
14. - Guevara
15. Devices for fishing
16. Prepare patient for operation
17. Soldiers
18. Laughing sound (2.2)
20. Ostrich-like birds
22. Spot on the skin
25. Golf peg
26. Maxim
27. Bawl
28. Greek goddess of the dawn
31. Scene of first miracle
32. Colorful form of the common carp
33. Upper respiratory tract infection
34. Before
35. The (German)
36. Blemish
37. Clumsy person
38. Something of tawdry design
39. Find out
42. Sensible
43. Shoemaker's tool
44. Large bay
46. Grate
50. Brown-capped boletus mushroom
51. Son of Isaac and Rebekah
52. Personalities
53. Bitter vetch
54. Storm
55. Delicatessen

DOWN
1. Scottish hill
2. Primate
3. Allow
4. Crazy
5. 1st letter of the Greek alphabet
6. Gambling game
7. Fish eggs
8. Fish-hawk
9. Pinnacle
10. Ostrich-like bird
11. Decades
19. Bullfight call
21. Masculine pronoun
22. Club-like weapon
23. 6th month of the Jewish calendar
24. Rattan
25. Prefix, three
27. Minced oath
28. Periods of history
29. Auricular
30. Hyperbolic sine
32. State of drowsy contentment
33. Spoke
35. Peril
36. Transgress
37. Otherwise
38. River in Zambia
39. Openwork fabric
40. Pitcher
41. Peaks
42. Metal dross
45. America (Abbr)
47. Mature
48. The sun
49. Pressure symbol

puzzle 27

ACROSS
1. Drugs
5. Skagen
9. Garment edge
12. In bed
13. Mother of Apollo
14. Bullfight call
15. Tie
16. Unique thing
17. Cabin
18. - Ono
20. Wild Asian dog
22. See
25. Witness
26. Stadium
27. Young goat
28. Monetary unit of Albania
31. Male deer
32. Policeman
33. Bound
34. Question
35. Actress, - Farrow
36. Difficult question
37. Brick carrier
38. Plunderer
39. Thresh
42. Fragments
43. Musical instrument
44. Blow-pipe missile
46. Dash
50. Not
51. Always
52. Ear part
53. Large barrel
54. Advise
55. Stringed toy

DOWN
1. Skilled
2. Japanese sash
3. Female swan
4. Swirling
5. Seaweed
6. Lotto-like gambling game
7. Dined
8. Phrased
9. Laughing sound (2.2)
10. 12th month of the Jewish calendar
11. Measure out
19. Wood sorrel
21. Masculine pronoun
22. U.S. space agency
23. Food scraps
24. Timber tree
25. Small drink
27. Hawaiian acacia
28. Was defeated
29. Fencing sword
30. Former Governor General, Sir John -
32. Spanish hero
33. Slackly
35. Crumble
36. Cooking implement
37. Hello there
38. Fluid measure
39. Baptismal vessel
40. Hawaiian feast
41. Capital of Yemen
42. Reared
45. Greeting
47. Card game
48. To endure
49. Prefix, new

puzzle 28

ACROSS
1. Require
5. Natter
9. Uncooked
12. Monster
13. Travelled on
14. Island (France)
15. Spur
16. Hautboy
17. Indicate assent
18. Remarkable
20. Finds shelter
22. Condiments
25. Prefix, whale
26. Menu
27. Prefix, before
28. Mineral spring
31. Greek god of war
32. Acknowledgement of debt
33. Hood-like membrane
34. An infusion
35. New Zealand bird
36. Unit of energy
37. Transgress
38. Pungent bulb plant
39. Chocolate powder
42. Canines
43. Monetary unit of Vietnam
44. Skagen
46. At sea
50. Exclamation of surprise
51. Flaky mineral
52. Large bay
53. Monetary unit of Afghanistan
54. Capital of Yemen
55. Send out

DOWN
1. Egg drink
2. The self
3. An age
4. Subtracts
5. Crocodiles (Colloq)
6. Tramp
7. Fuss
8. Titter
9. Skin
10. Agave
11. Marries
19. Born
21. Neuter singular pronoun
22. Shoo
23. River in central Switzerland
24. Fertiliser
25. French vineyard
27. Price on application (Abbr)
28. First king of Israel
29. Hungarian sheepdog
30. Smart - , show-off
32. Charged particle
33. Small bouquet
35. Poisonous effluvia
36. Sharp projection
37. Therefore
38. Daisy
39. A bloke
40. Island of Hawaii
41. Ember
42. Fresh-water fish
45. Young goat
47. Total
48. Biblical high priest
49. Nautical, rear

puzzle 29

ACROSS
1. Plays on words
5. Expectorate
9. Definite article
12. Tennis star, - Natase
13. Robust
14. Paddle
15. Sicilian volcano
16. Smart - , show-off
17. To and -
18. Torch
20. Dull sounds
22. Rummage
25. Prompt
26. Grassy plain
27. Scottish cap
28. Greek letter
31. Brink
32. Jack in cribbage
33. Heraldry, wide horizontal stripe on shield
34. Donkey
35. - Kelly
36. Camp shelters
37. Female deer
38. Persian musical instrument
39. Tramps
42. Prompted
43. Mature
44. Railed public transport
46. Engrave with acid
50. Sick
51. Italian capital
52. Uncommon
53. Soak flax
54. The maple
55. Reeled

DOWN
1. Pastry item
2. Last month
3. A fool
4. Shipping route (3,4)
5. Disgrace
6. Insect feeler
7. Island (France)
8. Rooflike structure
9. Beancurd
10. Difficult
11. Greek god of love
19. In the past
21. Masculine pronoun
22. Parasitic insect
23. One's parents (Colloq)
24. Torn clothing
25. Taxi
27. Fox
28. Camp shelter
29. Italian wine province
30. Former Soviet Union
32. Born
33. Automobile wheelguards
35. Cosa -, American Mafia
36. - kwon do (Korean martial art)
37. Perform
38. Ancient region in S Mesopotamia
39. Tress
40. Leer
41. Leather strap
42. Arrived
45. Fabulous bird
47. Faucet
48. French vineyard
49. Female bird

puzzle 30

ACROSS
1. Sound of a cat
5. Indian pulses
9. Mineral spring
12. Jaguarundi
13. Split
14. Brine-cured salmon
15. Measure out
16. Double curve
17. Land measure
18. Hyperbolic sine
20. Less cooked
22. Spiral formation
25. Monetary unit of Japan
26. Smart - , show-offs
27. Last letter
28. Bend
31. Subside
32. Acne pimple
33. Death rattle
34. Young child
35. Brown-capped boletus mushroom
36. Church walkway
37. Actress, - West
38. Accident
39. Black bird
42. Red planet
43. Biblical high priest
44. Indian nursemaid
46. Musical work
50. Cheat
51. Hang
52. Italian currency
53. New Zealand parrot
54. Sewing case
55. Sicilian volcano

DOWN
1. 13th letter of the Hebrew alphabet
2. Optic organ
3. Food scrap
4. Alas
5. Male bee
6. Lofty
7. Greeting
8. Ogled
9. Cabbage salad
10. Skin opening
11. Woodman
19. Sexless things
21. Prefix meaning without
22. Extensive
23. Potpourri
24. Time of abstinence
25. Become firm
27. Toothed fastener
28. Hit hard
29. Earthen pot
30. Sob
32. Letter Z
33. Meatball
35. Hors d'oeuvre
36. Atmosphere
37. Objective case of I
38. Muslim messiah
39. To matter
40. Agave
41. Musical instrument of India
42. Hindu lawgiver
45. To date
47. Mine
48. Vase
49. Large body of water

puzzle 31

ACROSS
1. Wax
5. Hawaiian goose
9. Room within a harem
12. Holly
13. Against
14. Cheat
15. Ceases living
16. Pool
17. An explosive
18. Drinking vessels
20. Consumption
22. Malign
25. Prefix, the earth
26. Spy
27. Assist
28. The (German)
31. Student at mixed school
32. Chest bone
33. German Mrs
34. Extrasensory perception
35. Mountain pass
36. Rub out
37. Part of a circle
38. Having nipples
39. Disgrace
42. Indonesian resort island
43. Very good (1-2)
44. Indian nursemaid
46. Scottish lake
50. Prefix, one
51. Serbian folk dance
52. Reverberate
53. Pet form of Leonard
54. Christmas
55. Incursion

DOWN
1. Spanish hero
2. Biblical high priest
3. Female ruff
4. Cut out
5. One of the two equal sections of a cone
6. Personalities
7. A fool
8. Invested
9. Prefix, eight
10. Hit or punch (Colloq)
11. Poker stake
19. Last month
21. Therefore
22. Sprint contest
23. Personalities
24. Vice president
25. Castrated male cat
27. Sicken
28. Minor oath
29. Relax
30. Regretted
32. Fabulous bird
33. More feeble
35. Dilapidated
36. Conger
37. Part of the verb "to be"
38. Lake in the Sierra Nevada
39. First king of Israel
40. Sharpen
41. Related
42. Formal dance
45. Yourself
47. Wood sorrel
48. Greek letter
49. Brick carrier

puzzle 32

ACROSS
1. Tasting like wild fowl
5. Stimulate
9. Girl (Slang)
12. Fencing sword
13. Islamic chieftain
14. The self
15. Allows
16. Edges
17. - Kelly
18. Tress
20. Ill-treat
22. Physician
25. Small truck
26. Pointed arch
27. Turkish cap
28. Jeer
31. Main island of Indonesia
32. Cove
33. College residential building
34. Room within a harem
35. Fish part
36. Solder
37. Fireplace ledge
38. Prayer
39. Founder of the Mogul Empire
42. Strike breaker
43. Regret
44. American state
46. Dull person
50. Anger
51. Extra
52. Lubricate
53. Clumsy person
54. Agitate
55. Gaelic

DOWN
1. Congeal
2. Primate
3. Greeted
4. Orthodox Jewish school
5. Prefix, sun
6. Primordial giant in Norse myth
7. Fruit seed
8. As a substitute
9. Knee
10. Matures
11. Ore deposit
19. Top card
21. To exist
22. Voodoo amulet
23. Minor oath
24. Prima donna
25. U-turn (Colloq)
27. Avid admirer
28. Large snakes
29. Ricelike grains of pasta
30. Portent
32. Infant's protective garment
33. Slobber
35. Tribunals
36. Brassiere
37. Masculine pronoun
38. Red earth pigment
39. Vigor
40. Subtle emanation
41. Cow flesh
42. Hindu garment
45. Young child
47. Of us
48. Observation
49. Female ruff

puzzle 33

ACROSS
1. Belly
5. Unit of computer memory
9. Part of a circle
12. Having wings
13. Paddles
14. Prefix, over
15. Prefix, foreign
16. Pare
17. The self
18. Cricketer, - Walters
20. Son of Abraham
22. Of apes
25. Prefix, the earth
26. Fall heavily
27. A craze
28. Vital tree fluid
31. Encircle
32. Which was to be proved
33. Robust
34. Legendary emperor of China
35. Prompt
36. Nurture
37. Monetary unit of Burma
38. Dray
39. Adapted to a dry environment
42. Angered
43. First woman
44. Stringed instrument
46. Cheat the system
50. Free
51. Inflammation (Suffix)
52. On top of
53. Aged
54. Girdle
55. Greet

DOWN
1. Bee product
2. Beer
3. Human race
4. Wearing
5. Boatswain
6. Yin and -
7. Prefix, three
8. Glimpsed
9. At sea
10. Wrinkle
11. Crocodile (Colloq)
19. Large tree
21. Therefore
22. Agile
23. Hip bones
24. Prefix, one
25. Goad for driving cattle
27. A charge
28. Hindu garment
29. As well as
30. Hammer head
32. As
33. Boring
35. Recurring in cycles
36. Not
37. The ratio between circumference and diameter
38. Plume
39. Prefix, dry
40. Sinister
41. Spawning area of salmon
42. Inflammation (Suffix)
45. Small truck
47. Open
48. Fish eggs
49. An explosive

puzzle 34

ACROSS
1. Small and cramped
5. Pare
9. To clothe
12. Agave
13. Vow
14. Primate
15. Long period of time
16. Bear constellation
17. Sheltered side
18. Glimpse
20. Shanty
22. Bondsmen
25. Letter Z
26. Fragrant flower
27. Sister
28. Once common, now banned, insecticide
31. Related
32. Item of headwear
33. Subtle emanation
34. Examine thoroughly
35. Doomed
36. Sicker
37. Peak
38. Fireplaces
39. Sordid
42. First class (1-3)
43. Sick
44. South African currency
46. Time of prosperity
50. Weir
51. Potpourri
52. Split
53. Abstract being
54. Small valley
55. Having wings

DOWN
1. Wages
2. Bullfight call
3. Hawaiian acacia
4. Capital of Armenia
5. Broths
6. Never
7. Sexless things
8. Stages
9. Monetary unit of Western Samoa
10. Oil cartel
11. Strange person
19. Dry (wine)
21. Masculine pronoun
22. European race
23. Prefer
24. Got down from mount
25. Toothed fastener
27. Utter
28. Lustreless
29. Endure
30. Sailors
32. Brown-capped boletus mushroom
33. Branch of mathematics
35. Fishing rod
36. Tavern
37. Part of the verb "to be"
38. Iodine solution
39. Team
40. Dash
41. Charity
42. Indigo
45. Beer
47. Lubricant
48. Eggs
49. Sea (French)

puzzle 35

ACROSS
1. Wildebeest
5. Pain
9. Eggs
12. Arouse
13. Move rapidly
14. Rummy game
15. - Lisa
16. Ocean fluctuation
17. Biblical high priest
18. Not kosher
20. Iron product
22. Madman
25. - de Janeiro
26. Black wood
27. Raises
28. British, a fool
31. Carolled
32. Garment edge
33. Team
34. Dined
35. Arable land temporarily sown with grass
36. Thrush
37. Female pig
38. Title for a woman
39. Arm joint
42. Chapter of the Koran
43. Expire
44. Little devils
46. Goddess of victory
50. Social insect
51. Ark builder
52. Hip bones
53. My, French (Plural)
54. Bloody
55. Monetary unit

DOWN
1. Gymnasium
2. Prefix, new
3. Vase
4. Performing on ice
5. Indian of Mexico
6. Skullcap
7. Brick carrier
8. Vomiting
9. Double curve
10. Evil
11. Indigo
19. Sunbeam
21. In the direction of
22. Rocky tableland
23. Adjoin
24. Not any
25. Rotational speed
27. U-turn (Colloq)
28. Suburb of Cairo
29. As previously given
30. Prefix, distant
32. Chop
33. Pertaining to the Sudan
35. Mooing
36. Paddle
37. Therefore
38. Pulpy
39. Dutch cheese
40. Row
41. Wagers
42. Mast
45. Cattle low
47. Island (France)
48. Relation
49. Consume

puzzle 36

ACROSS
1. Mongolian desert
5. Make indistinct
9. Which was to be proved
12. Metal spike
13. Relax
14. Small truck
15. Incite
16. Clutch
17. Dined
18. Decorated cake
20. Tool for boring holes
22. Sacred shrine
25. Sexless things
26. Singing group
27. Beer
28. Wager
31. Red planet
32. Noah's vessel
33. Conceal
34. Moose
35. Ballpoint biro
36. Black and white Chinese animal
37. - Kelly
38. Not very often
39. Ruffle
42. Rage
43. Bullfight call
44. Pastry item
46. Got down from mount
50. Monetary unit of Japan
51. River in central Europe
52. Sprint contest
53. - up, excited
54. Roster
55. Changed colour of

DOWN
1. Wildebeest
2. Paddle
3. Large
4. Inflammation of the ileum
5. Adorn with precious stones
6. Fat
7. America (Abbr)
8. Discount
9. Quagmire
10. Suffix, diminutive
11. Antlered beast
19. Worthless dog
21. Objective case of we
22. Pinnacle
23. Indian pulses
24. Royal House
25. Family
27. Part of a circle
28. Tie
29. Root of the taro
30. Side
32. Assist
33. Line for hoisting a sail
35. Person who bets
36. Each
37. Negative vote
38. Hindu scripture
39. Good-natured banter
40. To the sheltered side
41. Crooked
42. Worry
45. Fuss
47. Secular
48. Freeze
49. Spread out for drying

puzzle 37

ACROSS
1. Delays
5. Decorate (Xmas tree)
9. Witness
12. Dutch cheese
13. Death rattle
14. Shady tree
15. Root of the taro
16. Small island
17. Biblical high priest
18. Slat
20. Heavy drinker
22. Oar
25. Fairy
26. Gravelly hillside
27. Bingo-like game
28. Drunkard
31. Scorch
32. Wine
33. Untidy person
34. Attempt
35. Insane
36. Monetary unit of Oman
37. Sol
38. Cold season
39. Jargon
42. Isn't
43. Colour
44. Untidy state
46. Nautical call
50. Conger
51. A Great Lake
52. Comrade
53. Secret agent
54. Back
55. Finishes

DOWN
1. Sheltered side
2. Sum
3. Goad for driving cattle
4. Burn without flame
5. Banal
6. Hasty
7. Sick
8. Fittingly
9. Ooze
10. Australian super-model
11. Islamic chieftain
19. Beer
21. Belonging to
22. Surreptitious, attention getting sound
23. The maple
24. Cart
25. An age
27. Concealed
28. Narrow aperture
29. Seep
30. Type of automatic gear selector (1-3)
32. Forefront
33. Capital of New Mexico
35. Pantomimist
36. Garbage can
37. Therefore
38. More sensible
39. Angers
40. Profound
41. Lazily
42. Largest continent
45. Before
47. Female bird
48. W.A. river
49. Affirmative response

puzzle 38

ACROSS
1. Marsh plant
5. High-class
9. Colorful form of the common carp
12. Double curve
13. Arm bone
14. Raises
15. South American weapon
16. Meat cut
17. Indian dish
18. One of the Disciples
20. Wild Asian dog
22. Shrinks from
25. Sheltered side
26. Decorate
27. Eccentric wheel
28. Change colour of
31. Greek island in the Aegean
32. Lad
33. Ale
34. Bitter vetch
35. Debutante
36. Feet parts
37. The sun
38. Oar
39. Singers
42. The Orient
43. Pastry item
44. Non-scientific studies
46. Little devils
50. Large body of water
51. Obtains
52. Ponder
53. Newt
54. Fencing sword
55. Redact

DOWN
1. Hold up
2. The self
3. Conger
4. Traders
5. Bodies of ruined ships
6. Agave
7. Prefix, one
8. Bicycle for two
9. Accolade
10. Iridescent gem
11. Small island
19. Vase
21. Masculine pronoun
22. Shaped mass of food
23. River in central Europe
24. Courts
25. Secular
27. Corn ear
28. Property title
29. Shout
30. Gaelic
32. Unit of loudness
33. The time a person goes to bed
35. Prescribed quantity of medicine
36. Owns
37. Therefore
38. Out of date
39. Church recess
40. Willing
41. Nipple
42. Suffix, diminutive
45. Corded fabric
47. Mire
48. Pressure symbol
49. Become firm

puzzle 39

ACROSS
1. Peruvian capital
5. Aborigine of Borneo
9. Is able to
12. Having wings
13. Prefix, air
14. New Guinea seaport
15. Prefix, foreign
16. Adventuress
17. Crude mineral
18. Employs
20. Downy duck
22. Slacken
25. Play division
26. Ancient
27. Noah's vessel
28. Battle
31. Competed
32. Newt
33. Delete (Printing)
34. Greek goddess of the dawn
35. Become firm
36. Bandaged
37. Unit of loudness
38. Mailed
39. Confused mixture of sounds
42. Ethereal
43. Open
44. Circular plate
46. On top of
50. A fool
51. Prefix, eight
52. Death rattle
53. Vapour
54. Hitler's autobiography, "- Kampf"
55. Root of the taro

DOWN
1. Slack
2. Island (France)
3. Human race
4. Stirred
5. Recite the Jewish prayers
6. Shouts of agreement
7. Limb
8. Currency unit of the Soviet Union
9. Lump of clay
10. River in central Switzerland
11. Never
19. Monetary unit of Japan
21. Neuter singular pronoun
22. Adore
23. Potpourri
24. Poems
25. Talent
27. Nautical, rear
28. Sobbed
29. To the sheltered side
30. Spawning area of salmon
32. Conger
33. Carnivorous marsupial
35. Not very often
36. Rocky peak
37. To exist
38. Hickory nut
39. Dull resonant sound
40. Capital of Western Samoa
41. Scottish hills
42. Italian wine province
45. Freeze
47. Cushion
48. Aged
49. Prefix, new

puzzle 40

ACROSS
1. Wristband
5. Gust
9. Actor, - Chaney
12. At sea
13. Rant
14. Chop
15. Howl
16. Egg-shaped
17. My, French (Plural)
18. Trigonometric function
20. Persian lords
22. Vocal organ of birds
25. Bind
26. Delays
27. Prohibit
28. Rumen
31. Friend
32. Prompt
33. Entry permit
34. Hive insect
35. Fox
36. Repast
37. Jeer
38. Trilby hat
39. Farewell
42. Seep
43. Normal
44. Dowels
46. Gratuity
50. An age
51. Days before
52. Norse god of thunder
53. Lair
54. Jaguarundi
55. Islamic chieftain

DOWN
1. Taxi
2. America (Abbr)
3. Not many
4. Treachery
5. New York city borough
6. Wash
7. Eggs
8. The vault of heaven
9. Tibetan monk
10. Beasts of burden
11. Scottish headland
19. - and outs, intricacies
21. Masculine pronoun
22. Mop
23. American university
24. Anger
25. - kwon do (Korean martial art)
27. Immature flower
28. Goodbye
29. Former Soviet Union
30. Information
32. Dove's call
33. Mounted sentry
35. Wig
36. Turkish cap
37. To exist
38. Cavity
39. Mimicked
40. Challenge
41. Republic in SW Asia
42. Unique thing
45. Climbing plant
47. Electrical resistance unit
48. Colorful form of the common carp
49. Go wrong

puzzle 41

ACROSS
1. Cosy
5. Object of worship
9. Thrash
12. Nobleman
13. Row
14. Beer
15. Hawaiian goose
16. Personalities
17. Victory sign
18. Nestling
20. Hit
22. Causing unity
25. "The Raven" author
26. Television repeat
27. Automobile
28. Piece
31. Implement
32. Lad
33. Nonsense
34. Tavern
35. Utter
36. Large violin-like instrument
37. Obtained
38. More daring
39. Wealthy person
42. Street of stabling
43. Paddle
44. Islamic chieftain
46. Bound
50. Land measure
51. Uncivil
52. Friend
53. Female bird
54. Struck
55. Advise

DOWN
1. Monetary unit of Japan
2. Not
3. Vase
4. Merry
5. Pertaining to the ileum
6. Excavates
7. Yoko -
8. Person who grants a lease
9. Molten rock
10. Smart - , show-off
11. Humble
19. - and Yang
21. Objective case of I
22. Upper respiratory tract infection
23. Lighting gas
24. Press clothes
25. Wages
27. Bashful
28. Daring
29. Small island
30. Norse god of thunder
32. Flying mammal
33. Communications satellite
35. Sir Garfield -, West Indian cricketer
36. Bovine
37. Depart
38. Tam
39. Ark builder
40. River in central Switzerland
41. Machine-gun
42. Skirt coming to just below knee
45. Mother
47. Island (France)
48. Antiquity
49. Change colour of

puzzle 42

ACROSS
1. Narcotics agent
5. Heed
9. - and outs, intricacies
12. Hip bones
13. Star in Lyra
14. New Guinea seaport
15. Clothesline clips
16. Great age
17. Anger
18. Young cow
20. Sound of a duck
22. Timber trees
25. Legal right
26. Dwelling
27. Garland
28. To clothe
31. Not any
32. Allow
33. Prong
34. An explosive
35. Monetary unit of Romania
36. Valleys
37. Transfix
38. Demure
39. Sponsorship
42. High-pitched tone
43. Is able to
44. Leg part
46. Merely
50. Mount - , N.W. Qld. mining town
51. Expression used when accident happens
52. Cut with laser
53. The (German)
54. Rocky tableland
55. Finishes

DOWN
1. Pinch
2. Beer
3. Outfit
4. Waterfall
5. Sportsgrounds
6. Cow flesh
7. The self
8. Yankee
9. Hip bones
10. Narcotics agent
11. Search for
19. Land measure
21. Objective case of we
22. Tilt
23. Black
24. Do not
25. Black
27. Monetary unit of Romania
28. Roofing slate
29. Single items
30. Romance tale
32. Pet form of Leonard
33. Young frog
35. Limber, supple
36. Female deer
37. The ratio between circumference and diameter
38. Altar stone
39. Etching fluid
40. Relax
41. Growl
42. Beeps horn
45. Gardening tool
47. Grandmother
48. Hallucinogenic drug
49. Affirmative response

puzzle 43

ACROSS
1. Grotto
5. Withered
9. Mineral spring
12. Fertiliser
13. On top of
14. Sphere
15. Wagers
16. Debutantes
17. Teenage lout
18. Relax
20. Consumption
22. Ephemerid
25. Prefix, the earth
26. In an entangled state
27. Cushion
28. Wager
31. Shopping centre
32. Young bear
33. Chapter of the Koran
34. Noah's vessel
35. Taxi
36. Revolves
37. Weir
38. Cavalry sword
39. Lure
42. Got down from mount
43. Mount - , N.W. Qld. mining town
44. Budge
46. Sea eagles
50. Dance step
51. Nautical, below
52. Lowest high tide
53. Take to court
54. Tidings
55. Refuse

DOWN
1. Young bear
2. Land measure
3. Examine thoroughly
4. Soothing
5. Resembling suds
6. Fencing sword
7. Hold up
8. Followed
9. Soybean
10. Forage
11. French clergyman
19. Everything
21. Therefore
22. Mother
23. Distant
24. Egg part
25. Talk
27. Hotel
28. Bindi-eye prickle
29. Sea eagle
30. Soviet news service
32. Eccentric wheel
33. Occur beneath
35. Alligator
36. - Chi. Slow moving martial art form
37. Perform
38. Swings to the side
39. Immerses
40. Son of Isaac and Rebekah
41. Instance
42. Confess
45. Bullfight call
47. Female ruff
48. Grandmother
49. Secret agent

puzzle 44

ACROSS
1. Beer (Colloq)
5. Certainly
9. Sulky
12. First class (1-3)
13. Bag
14. Japanese sash
15. South African
16. Region
17. Unit of loudness
18. Madam
20. Betwixt
22. Jewish
25. Letter Z
26. African antelope
27. In favour of
28. Firearm
31. Poker stake
32. In favour of
33. Polynesian root food
34. Not
35. In favour of
36. Sponsorship
37. 3 Thickness
38. Entwine
39. Shinbone
42. Appends
43. Fuss
44. Carolled
46. Captured
50. Last month
51. Measure out
52. Land measure
53. An infusion
54. Affirmative votes
55. Ostrich-like bird

DOWN
1. Talk
2. Kangaroo
3. Monad
4. Relevant
5. Son of Abraham
6. Fairly hot
7. Freeze
8. Performer on ice
9. Mongolian desert
10. Mountain goat
11. Golden
19. Assist
21. Plural of I
22. Sturdy twilled fabric
23. Arm bone
24. An appointment
25. Menagerie
27. To and -
28. Insane
29. Of urine
30. Proboscis
32. Snoop
33. Communications satellite
35. Blood fluid
36. Also
37. The ratio between circumference and diameter
38. Borders
39. Tense
40. Lazy
41. Goatskin bag for holding wine
42. Poker stake
45. U-turn (Colloq)
47. Scottish expression
48. Crude mineral
49. New Zealand parrot

puzzle 45

ACROSS
1. Yin and -
5. Goatskin bag for holding wine
9. Flying mammal
12. Agave
13. Military detachment
14. The self
15. Female birds
16. Depend
17. Fish eggs
18. Sailors
20. Sharp ringing sounds
22. Shrews
25. Transfix
26. Oneness
27. Dry (wine)
28. However
31. Land measure
32. Knight's title
33. Cut with laser
34. Female deer
35. Affirmative response
36. Card game
37. An infusion
38. Reddish-brown hair
39. Disorder
42. Long fish
43. Exclamation of wonder
44. Brief note
46. Weary
50. Yoko -
51. Related
52. Redact
53. Unlocking implement
54. Devices for fishing
55. Hindu music

DOWN
1. Exclamation of disgust
2. Beer
3. Prefix, not
4. Develop slowly
5. Bindi-eye prickles
6. Single items
7. Sesame plant
8. Abnormal
9. Capital of Switzerland
10. Eager
11. Pedal digits
19. Some
21. Prefix meaning not
22. Quadrangle
23. Remarkable
24. Ireland
25. Each
27. Sister
28. Capital of Azerbaijan
29. Consumer
30. Sea bird
32. Large body of water
33. Marine crustacean
35. Sycophant
36. Monetary unit of Afghanistan
37. In the direction of
38. Ages
39. Prepare food
40. Sharpen
41. Nautical call
42. Send out
45. Supplement existence
47. Highest mountain in Crete
48. Outfit
49. Greek letter

puzzle 46

ACROSS
1. Agreement
5. Crustacean
9. Forefront
12. Unique thing
13. Hindu music
14. The self
15. Suffix, diminutive
16. Once again
17. Acknowledgement of debt
18. Follower of Hitler
20. Stoppers
22. Hawk goods
25. Yes
26. Rain and snow
27. Tiny
28. Monetary unit of Romania
31. Toboggan
32. Bleat
33. Cots
34. Spread out for drying
35. Sly animal
36. Rocky heights
37. Lad
38. Gardening tool
39. Five pound note
42. Father
43. Monad
44. Greg Norman's sport
46. Notes at scale's ends
50. Freeze
51. Fencing sword
52. Siamese
53. Fold
54. Precious
55. Brick carriers

DOWN
1. "The Raven" author
2. Social insect
3. Prefix, whale
4. Tended
5. Derange
6. Indian queen
7. Mature
8. Old Scottish bullion coin
9. Streak of ore
10. Eager
11. Commonsense
19. High-pitched
21. Toward the top
22. Surreptitious, attention getting sound
23. Australian super-model
24. Property title
25. Yes
27. Bee product
28. Heavy metal
29. Brink
30. Former Soviet Union
32. Lad
33. Width
35. Counterfeited
36. Brown-capped boletus mushroom
37. To exist
38. A sacrament
39. Thwart
40. Ancient Peruvian
41. Vice president
42. Prayer
45. Open
47. Exclamation of surprise
48. Possessed
49. Sister

puzzle 47

ACROSS
1. Mature
5. Monetary unit of Angola
9. Fly larva
12. Beaten by tennis service
13. Prefix, air
14. Observation
15. Abominable snowman
16. Marsh plant
17. New Zealand bird
18. Small nail
20. Card game for three
22. Diocese
25. Regret
26. Ladle
27. Long-leaved lettuce
28. Castrated male cat
31. Avoid
32. A month
33. Green stone
34. 9th letter of the Hebrew alphabet
35. Brown shade
36. Money
37. Male offspring
38. Renowned
39. Lively dance
42. Ornamental brooch
43. Kangaroo
44. Fishing reel
46. Upper respiratory tract infection
50. - and outs, intricacies
51. Dash
52. Christmas
53. Born
54. Depend
55. Timber tree

DOWN
1. Sunbeam
2. Freeze
3. Domesticated animal
4. Particular printing of book
5. Coniferous tree
6. Seven days
7. Before
8. Pertaining to iodine
9. Explosive device
10. Hautboy
11. Russian emperor
19. Egyptian serpent
21. Objective case of I
22. Surreptitious, attention getting sound
23. Pain
24. Disorderly flight
25. - Rene. Mo
27. Is able to
28. Jail
29. Lazy
30. Necklace component
32. Human race
33. Seek employment
35. Top hat
36. Raincoat
37. Therefore
38. Amusing
39. Smile
40. First class (1-3)
41. Be defeated
42. Spoken
45. Island (France)
47. Fish eggs
48. An infusion
49. Family

puzzle 48

ACROSS
1. Mound
5. Boss on a shield
9. Nave
12. At sea
13. Search for
14. Mature
15. Yin and -
16. One of Columbus's ships
17. Island (France)
18. Paradise
20. Coral builder
22. Open shelter
25. Transfix
26. Spy
27. Vapour
28. Hallucinogenic drug
31. A man
32. Piece
33. Grain store
34. Sum
35. Crane boom
36. A cold
37. Twosome
38. Pursues
39. Wealthy person
42. Nourishment
43. Female sheep
44. Bindi-eye prickle
46. Information
50. Talent
51. Islamic call to prayer
52. Wyatt -
53. Handwoven Scandinavian rug
54. Coxae
55. Indian peasant

DOWN
1. Cattle fodder
2. America (Abbr)
3. Soldiers
4. Spectacle
5. Pale green mosslike lichen
6. Hitler's autobiography, "- Kampf"
7. Scottish hill
8. Giraffe-like animals
9. Greet
10. Unattractive
11. High-pitched tone
19. Once common, now banned, insecticide
21. Not off
22. Hindu music
23. Old
24. Repair
25. Dab
27. Castrated male cat
28. Falsehoods
29. Swing around
30. Benedictine monks' titles
32. Prefix, life
33. More protected from sun
35. Moslem robe
36. 17th letter of the Greek alphabet
37. Perform
38. Cures with brine
39. Close to
40. Askew
41. Greek letter
42. Bind securely (Nautical)
45. Israeli submachine gun
47. No
48. To and -
49. Choose

puzzle 49

ACROSS
1. Haul
5. Crook
9. Become firm
12. U.S. State
13. French clergyman
14. Avail of
15. Staffs
16. Nuisance
17. New Guinea seaport
18. Bulb flower
20. Loose fiber used for caulking
22. Appease
25. Donkey
26. Images
27. Cereal
28. Monetary unit of Romania
31. Prude
32. Primate
33. Drunkards
34. Monetary unit of Japan
35. Rotational speed
36. Ravels
37. Remove intestines from fish
38. Inchworm
39. Ravine
42. Ursa
43. Charged particle
44. Capital of Norway
46. Type of automatic gear selector (1-3)
50. Attempt
51. On top of
52. Relax
53. Gender
54. Stable attendant
55. Levee

DOWN
1. Beetle
2. 17th letter of the Greek alphabet
3. Assist
4. Young goose
5. Perhaps
6. Heed
7. Observation
8. Monosaccharide
9. Peevish fit
10. Son of Isaac and Rebekah
11. Abound
19. Possibilities
21. Similar to
22. Fruit seeds
23. Land measure
24. Piece of money
25. Affirmative vote
27. Rotational speed
28. Noose
29. Suffix, diminutive
30. Former Soviet Union
32. Fitting
33. Grunted
35. Tinged with red
36. Hawaiian acacia
37. Depart
38. Monetary unit of Sierra Leone
39. Packs
40. Tradition
41. Variety of chalcedony
42. Political combine
45. Secret agent
47. Cove
48. Question
49. Female ruff

puzzle 50

ACROSS
1. Garden tool
5. Prayer ending
9. That woman
12. Oil cartel
13. Mother of Apollo
14. Breakfast cereal
15. Freshwater duck
16. Amphibian
17. Ignited
18. In a line
20. Wild Asian dog
22. One-armed bandits (Colloq)
25. Female ruff
26. River in W Canada
27. Free
28. Skilled
31. Old cloth measures
32. Fruit seed
33. Hick
34. Farewell
35. Chafe
36. Acted silently
37. Name
38. Jabber
39. Disorder
42. 11th president of the U.S
43. Exclamation of wonder
44. Informed
46. Near
50. Jeer
51. Fencing sword
52. Notion
53. Firmament
54. Something owing
55. In -, in all

DOWN
1. Decay
2. Primate
3. New Zealand parrot
4. Chocolate and cream delicacies
5. Singers
6. Sound of a cat
7. Greek letter
8. Inclined head
9. Performance by one
10. Greet
11. Suffix, diminutive
19. Colour
21. Masculine pronoun
22. Plebeian
23. Greasy
24. Cabbagelike plant
25. Tear
27. Chest bone
28. Mute
29. Cain's victim
30. English monk
32. Hotel
33. Knitted pattern
35. Oxidised
36. - de mer, seasickness
37. Perform
38. Triangular insert
39. Male swans
40. Crook
41. Nautical call
42. Plebeian
45. Open
47. Revised form of Esperanto
48. Obtain
49. Monetary unit of Vietnam

puzzle 51

ACROSS
1. Part of the verb "to be"
3. Merrily
7. Unwinds
9. Prefix meaning not
11. Seasoning
12. Fuss
13. Near to
15. Objective case of we
16. Also
17. Pedal digit
19. Agitate
21. Wallaroo
23. Fire remains
24. Automobile
25. Toward the top
27. Masculine pronoun
28. Vapour
29. Russian emperor
31. Not off
32. Own
34. Watcher
35. Perform

DOWN
1. Prefix meaning without
2. Missus
3. Sets
4. High-pitched
5. Part of the verb to be
6. Language of European Jews
7. Salt of uric acid
8. French, water
10. Negative vote
12. Rectangular pier
14. Enormously-beaked tropical American birds
16. Similar to
18. Periods of history
20. Ostrich-like birds
22. Otherwise
25. Former Soviet Union
26. Dance step
28. Depart
29. Pedal digit
30. Colour
32. The ratio between circumference and diameter
33. Therefore

puzzle 52

ACROSS
1. Not off
3. Father of Leah and Rachel
7. Stringed instrument
9. Objective case of we
11. Restrain
12. Revised form of Esperanto
13. Prefix meaning not
15. Perform
16. Pig
17. Meadow
19. Certainly
21. Old cloth measures
23. Black bird
24. Cracker biscuit
25. Depart
27. Depart
28. Rocky peak
29. Bungle
31. Not off
32. Netherlands queen
34. Outlay
35. Prefix meaning without

DOWN
1. Satisfactory
2. Gist
3. Mother of Apollo
4. Beer
5. To exist
6. Elbowing
7. Useful
8. Boy
10. Therefore
12. U.S. State
14. Wrestling holds
16. Hello there
18. Having wings
20. American Indian
22. Therefore
25. Pleased
26. Not at home
28. In the direction of
29. Marsh
30. Brassiere
32. To exist
33. Prefix meaning not

puzzle 53

ACROSS
1. Belonging to
3. Hazy
7. Mosquito (Colloq)
9. Prefix meaning without
11. Temple
12. 17th letter of the Greek alphabet
13. Objective case of we
15. Toward the top
16. Haul
17. Female sheep
19. Exclude
21. Delicatessen
23. Pressure symbol
24. High-pitched
25. Not off
27. Objective case of I
28. Dined
29. In a line
31. Objective case of I
32. Identity discs (3,4)
34. Frequented by rooks
35. Therefore

DOWN
1. Satisfactory
2. Marsh
3. Halt
4. My, French (Plural)
5. Otherwise
6. Worship of Yahweh
7. Veered
8. French, water
10. Negative vote
12. Gambol
14. Knitted jacket
16. In the direction of
18. Australian super-model
20. Rows
22. Neuter singular pronoun
25. Wild revelry
26. Negating word
28. Part of the verb "to be"
29. Very good (1-2)
30. Once existed
32. Perform
33. Depart

puzzle 54

ACROSS
1. Objective case of I
3. Australian marsupial
7. Sharp-sighted
9. Depart
11. Double on a bicycle (Colloq)
12. Wine
13. In the direction of
15. Perform
16. Take a seat
17. Carp-like fish
19. Egg-shaped
21. Maize
23. Dined
24. - de Janeiro
25. Plural of I
27. Bovine beast
28. A dynasty in China
29. Shape
31. Prefix meaning not
32. Social outcasts
34. Dense
35. To exist

DOWN
1. Possessive form of me
2. Finish
3. Lotto-like gambling game
4. Large tree
5. Prefix meaning without
6. Restless (music)
7. Living in flowing water
8. Spanish hero
10. Not off
12. Exclamation of acclaim
14. Odorous substance
16. Therefore
18. Ireland
20. Lexicon
22. Negative vote
25. Toil
26. Biblical high priest
28. Hello there
29. Raincoat
30. Skilled
32. The ratio between circumference and diameter
33. Masculine pronoun

puzzle 55

ACROSS
1. Part of the verb "to be"
3. Muslim messiah
7. Spiritual interpretation
9. Negative vote
11. - Ono
12. Question
13. Belonging to
15. To exist
16. Atomic mass unit
17. Tibetan ox
19. Yugoslavian
21. Close hard
23. Prefix, new
24. Firmament
25. Perform
27. Perform
28. - Maria, coffee liqueur
29. Decant
31. Belonging to
32. Hindu religious retreats
34. Abominable snowmen
35. Plural of I

DOWN
1. Prefix meaning without
2. A month
3. Donkey
4. In the past
5. Masculine pronoun
6. Made sure
7. Nautical calls
8. Sailor
10. Satisfactory
12. Prayer ending
14. Fraudulently alter
16. Similar to
18. New Zealand parrot
20. Volumes
22. Possessive form of me
25. Notes at scale's ends
26. Of us
28. In the direction of
29. Pressure symbol
30. Uncooked
32. Near to
33. Objective case of I

puzzle 56

ACROSS
1. Turkish governor
4. Monetary unit of Angola
8. Sick
11. Mountain goat
13. Great age
14. Regret
15. Type of automatic gear selector (1-3)
16. Inhabitant of Canada
18. Cavalry sword
20. Effort
21. Actor
23. Energy
24. U-turn (Colloq)
25. Leather whip
27. Surreptitious, attention getting sound
31. Pace
33. An infusion
34. Christmas
35. Israeli round dance
36. Long fish
38. Flee
39. Hallucinogenic drug
41. Ticked
43. Norwegian dramatist
46. Waned
47. Forced high notes
49. Wallaroo
52. Influenza
53. Floor covering
54. Old injury mark
55. Your (Colloq)
56. Lose water
57. Russian secret police

DOWN
1. Piece
2. Wane
3. Sycophant
4. Torn
5. Erode
6. An age
7. Vapid
8. Eye part
9. Hawaiian feast
10. Telescope part
12. Photograph of bones (1-3)
17. Foolish
19. Wager
21. Jostle
22. Mother of Apollo
23. Psalter
26. Tiny
28. Scoter
29. Swing around
30. Nurse
32. Fades
37. Kinsman
40. Fishhook line
42. Professional charges
43. Full of unresolved questions
44. Wool package
45. Elide
46. Sicilian volcano
48. Bind
50. Tatter
51. Sphere

puzzle 57

ACROSS
1. Benedictine monk's title
4. Type of inflorescence
8. Bleat
11. Nautical call
13. Great age
14. Haul
15. Exploding star
16. Beautiful, seductive spy (4.4)
18. Sea eagles
20. Havana resident
21. Hollow-nosed bullet
23. Sexless things
24. Monad
25. Type of automatic gear selector (1-3)
27. Gaiter
31. Trigonometric function
33. Go wrong
34. Practitioner of yoga
35. Suffix, diminutive
36. Riding strap
38. Take to court
39. Decay
41. Sway
43. Blemish
46. Wearied
47. Chair for two persons
49. Cut with laser
52. The self
53. Roof overhang
54. Short take-off and landing aircraft
55. Ashen
56. Type of jazz
57. Finish

DOWN
1. Level of karate proficiency
2. Exclamation of surprise
3. Motion
4. Soft cheese
5. Shouts of agreement
6. Witty remark
7. Make law
8. Reveal secret
9. Subtle emanation
10. Against
12. Length measure
17. Lewd woman
19. Hard-shelled fruit
21. Measure of medicine
22. Military detachment
23. Vexed
26. Land measure
28. Follow in time
29. Fever
30. Row
32. Weird
37. - Kelly
40. Beginning
42. Long fish
43. Swing to the side
44. Roman garment
45. Shakespeare's river
46. Main island of Indonesia
48. Otic organ
50. Male offspring
51. Antiquity

puzzle 58

ACROSS
1. Garbage can
4. Poet
8. Metal rod
11. Got down from mount
13. Potpourri
14. Yoko -
15. Sand dune
16. Conferences
18. Soother
20. The end
21. Brawl
23. Hallucinogenic drug
24. Zodiac sign
25. Capital of Norway
27. Periods of history
31. Prefix, distant
33. That woman
34. Anger
35. One's parents (Colloq)
36. Chances
38. Tibetan gazelle
39. However
41. A parent
43. Of bees
46. City in central Belgium
47. Third
49. Distant
52. Crude mineral
53. Threesome
54. Hick
55. My, French (Plural)
56. Long period of time
57. Soap ingredient

DOWN
1. Evil
2. Island (France)
3. Nine times as much
4. Golfing stroke resulting in one over par (5.4)
5. Having wings
6. Chest bone
7. Takes off (clothes)
8. Boatswain
9. Against
10. Antarctic explorer
12. Rip
17. Downy duck
19. Cracker biscuit
21. Singer
22. Sense
23. Chief municipal officer
26. Captained
28. Having a just claim
29. Agave
30. Scorch
32. Convocation of witches
37. The sun
40. Oneness
42. Russian emperor
43. Small particle
44. Father
45. Angers
46. Opera solo
48. Land measure
50. To endure
51. Female ruff

puzzle 59

ACROSS
1. Cooking implement
4. Cloak
8. Sphere
11. Ireland
13. Crude minerals
14. Monetary unit of Afghanistan
15. Stage show
16. Capital of Chile
18. Bread particle
20. Applause
21. Worldly goods
23. In favour of
24. Prefix, one
25. English college
27. Soft lambskin leather
31. Part played
33. I have
34. Strike breaker
35. Heed
36. Hood-like membrane
38. French vineyard
39. Egos
41. French dance
43. Make amends
46. Emirate on the Persian Gulf
47. Sumerian temple tower
49. Conceited
52. Bullfight call
53. Basic monetary unit of Ghana
54. Sicilian volcano
55. Victory sign
56. Heroic
57. Supplement existence

DOWN
1. Energy
2. Lubricant
3. Ductile
4. Makeup
5. Semite
6. Female swan
7. Chemical compound
8. Iridescent gem
9. Wrinkle
10. Ink stain
12. Jaguarundi
17. Images
19. Small truck
21. Wallaroo
22. Scorning person
23. Pertaining to air
26. Eggs
28. Free from error
29. Shave
30. Adjoin
32. Watching
37. Ignited
40. Tennis score
42. Wheel hub
43. Northern arm of the Black Sea
44. Roofing slate
45. Double curve
46. Muslim judge
48. Corded fabric
50. Writing fluid
51. Not

puzzle 60

ACROSS
1. Carp-like fish
4. Scorch
8. Norse goddess
11. Arrive
13. Tempt
14. Room within a harem
15. Long period of time
16. The treatment of cancer
18. Nest
20. Jabs
21. Tilted
23. Pig enclosure
24. Play division
25. Sky colour
27. Islamic call to prayer
31. Prepare patient for operation
33. Doctrine
34. Tradition
35. Jostle
36. New Zealand parrots
38. Wood sorrel
39. Beer
41. Zero
43. Effervescent
46. Mine excavation
47. Clerisy
49. Unique thing
52. Poem
53. Executive Officer
54. Near
55. 13th letter of the Hebrew alphabet
56. Hardens
57. Dove's call

DOWN
1. Gelid
2. Female deer
3. Issues
4. Nebulose
5. Vandals
6. Part of a circle
7. Re-choose
8. Crook
9. Brink
10. Puts down
12. Ireland
17. Faithful
19. Debutante
21. Scandinavian
22. Colour of unbleached linen
23. Semasiology
26. Avail of
28. Caused by animals
29. Curved entrance
30. Tidy
32. Stage
37. Cracker biscuit
40. Harp-like instruments
42. On top of
43. Glimpse
44. Assistant
45. Stalk
46. Printer's mark, keep
48. Chop
50. The self
51. 17th letter of the Greek alphabet

puzzle 61

ACROSS
1. Poke
4. Indian pulses
8. Rotational speed
11. Image
13. Christmas
14. Acknowledgement of debt
15. Knee
16. Railway ties
18. Cub leader
20. Breathes rattlingly
21. Exhausted
23. Affirmative vote
24. Biblical high priest
25. The maple
27. Curved entrance
31. Burden
33. Label
34. African river
35. Oblique
36. Angered
38. Cloistered woman
39. Etcetera
41. Pokes with elbow
43. Capital of Ghana
46. Place
47. Capital of Finland
49. Bull
52. Crude mineral
53. Walk
54. Level
55. Evergreen tree
56. Poker stake
57. First woman

DOWN
1. Lively dance
2. Top card
3. Authentic
4. One who has a reading ability impairment
5. Hawaiian dance
6. Beer
7. Wary
8. Monetary unit of Cambodia
9. Skin opening
10. Rumple
12. Use atomic bom on (Colloq)
17. Song of praise
19. Greek letter
21. Long fish
22. Antiaircraft fire
23. Silver sulfide
26. Otic organ
28. Small domestic dove
29. A hint
30. Female birds
32. Pitchers
37. Owing
40. Coniferous evergreen forest
42. An appointment
43. Nautical call
44. Wax
45. Skein of thread
46. Short parody
48. Grandmother
50. Speed up motor
51. Monad

puzzle 62

ACROSS
1. Affirmative vote
4. Spinning toys
8. In the past
11. A burden
13. Norse god
14. Dog's foot
15. Luxuriant
16. Envoy's office
18. Potato (Colloq)
20. Embers
21. Bawler
23. Supplement existence
24. Exclamation of surprise
25. Exclamations of surprise
27. Vow
31. Flame
33. Beep horn
34. Hindu god of destruction
35. Bustle or fuss (Colloq) (2-2)
36. Welsh emblem
38. Small bird
39. That woman
41. Entertain
43. Cleaning lady
46. Doughnut-shaped roll
47. A seric
49. Near
52. Very good (1-2)
53. Circular plate
54. Portico
55. Farewell
56. W.A. eucalypt
57. Sweet potato

DOWN
1. Everything
2. Yourself
3. Towards the orient
4. Able to be put up with
5. River in central Europe
6. Hog
7. Light meal
8. Capital of Western Samoa
9. Jail
10. 3 Admits
12. Indian pulses
17. New Guinea currency units
19. An infusion
21. Handle of a knife
22. U.S. State
23. Western Australian coastal town
26. Hasten
28. Vigor
29. Sinister
30. Assess
32. Red dye
37. Beer barrel
40. Intoxicating
42. Clan
43. Strike breaker
44. Nautical call
45. Levee
46. Strong woody fiber
48. Actress, - Farrow
50. Tibetan gazelle
51. Overact

puzzle 63

ACROSS
1. Embrace
4. Slide
8. Printer's measures
11. Once again
13. Fleet rodent
14. Actress, - Farrow
15. Small spider
16. Choosing
18. Muddle
20. Eagle's nest
21. Descriptive of a house built on a concrete slab
23. Possibilities
24. Eggs
25. Long fish
27. South-east Asian nation
31. States
33. - de Janeiro
34. Land measure
35. Otherwise
36. Brink
38. Road surfacing
39. Marry
41. Star (Heraldry)
43. Seraph
46. The elbow
47. Military dictator
49. Gist
52. Belonging to him
53. Ballet skirt
54. Chapter of the Koran
55. Newt
56. Personalities
57. Among

DOWN
1. Overact
2. Prefix, one
3. Escapes
4. Protected
5. Cabbagelike plant
6. Anger
7. Decaffeinated
8. Islamic chieftain
9. Short dress
10. Wise
12. Marries
17. Unit of magnetic induction
19. Scottish river
21. Be defeated
22. Egg-shaped
23. Having the same origin
26. Bottle top
28. Radioactive metallic element
29. Spoken
30. Withered
32. Stitched
37. Etcetera
40. The cream
42. Expression used when accident happens
43. Pain
44. Naive person
45. Sudden blow
46. Singer
48. Haul
50. Prefix, three
51. Possessed

puzzle 64

ACROSS
1. Tibetan ox
4. Monetary unit of Angola
8. Ethnic telecaster
11. Send out
13. Nobleman
14. Not
15. Naked
16. Preparation for killing algae
18. Knot
20. Tout
21. Trafalgar hero
23. Atomic mass unit
24. Fuss
25. Monarch
27. Levels of karate proficiency
31. Rescue
33. Prefix, new
34. Son of Isaac and Rebekah
35. Prayer ending
36. Hereditary factor
38. Knight's title
39. Donkey
41. Emphatic form of it
43. Draw forth
46. Hymn
47. Likeness of a person
49. Capable
52. Highest mountain in Crete
53. Monetary unit of Peru
54. Merriment
55. Mountain pass
56. Exchequer
57. - and Yang

DOWN
1. Japanese currency
2. Atomic mass unit
3. Glove made of kid leather
4. One's acquired knowledge
5. Building side
6. Work unit
7. Hipbone
8. Drag logs
9. Past tense of bid
10. Prophet
12. Decades
17. Unrefined
19. Very good (1-2)
21. U.S. space agency
22. Dutch cheese
23. Combative
26. Born
28. Gathering
29. Metal spike
30. Breakers
32. Make law
37. Greek letter
40. Letter cross-line
42. Metal dross
43. Heroic
44. Extinct bird
45. European mountain range
46. Mines
48. Black bird
50. Garland
51. Even (poet.)

puzzle 65

ACROSS
1. Kangaroo
4. Woe is me
8. Work unit
11. Paradise
13. Murky
14. Pastry item
15. Glass panel
16. Devotion to the humanities
18. Rowed
20. Doesn't have
21. Hesitate
23. Axlike tool
24. Fuss
25. Freshwater duck
27. Officiating priest of a mosque
31. Excavates
33. Zero
34. Wise
35. Eye inflammation
36. Crustacean
38. Cloistered woman
39. "The Raven" author
41. Secretly attacked
43. Papua and New Guinea river
46. Major artery
47. Indonesian volcano
49. Send out
52. - and Yang
53. Pornography (Colloq)
54. Greatly
55. Abstract being
56. Angered
57. Witness

DOWN
1. Corded fabric
2. Room within a harem
3. Science of winemaking
4. Allegiance
5. Praise
6. Limb
7. Scandinavian poet
8. Heroic
9. Endanger
10. Jewels
12. Tidy
17. Hitler's followers
19. Soak flax
21. Crazes
22. Entrance
23. Versatile
26. Atmosphere
28. A superior court writ
29. Fever
30. Repair
32. Papua and New Guinea river
37. Metal rod
40. Giraffe-like animal
42. A particular
43. Inner Hebrides island
44. Ireland
45. Kitchen utensils
46. River in central Switzerland
48. Rocky peak
50. Freeze
51. Definite article

puzzle 66

ACROSS
1. Bitter vetch
4. Supplements
8. That woman
11. Large trees
13. Prefix, dry
14. Battle
15. Russian no
16. Seaport on W Kyushu
18. The east wind
20. Small dogs
21. Short, light sleep
23. Pressure symbol
24. Beer
25. Egyptian deity
27. Naive person
31. Uncommon
33. Revised form of Esperanto
34. Otherwise
35. Former
36. Italian wine province
38. Falsehood
39. Norse goddess
41. Most senior
43. Bulb vegetable
46. Spread
47. Scoundrel
49. Driving shower
52. Haul
53. Jot
54. Detest
55. Black bird
56. Absent
57. Golf peg

DOWN
1. An age
2. Sunbeam
3. Mosquitoes (Colloq)
4. Outside marriage
5. New Zealand parrots
6. Work unit
7. Lathers
8. Sealed with a kiss
9. Codlike fish
10. Greek goddess of strife
12. Daze
17. Fishing net
19. Knock with knuckles
21. Attention
22. Having wings
23. Screenplay
26. Commercials
28. Cat of unknown parentage
29. Egyptian goddess of fertility
30. Length measures
32. Spirit
37. Sick
40. Abstract beings
42. Sprint
43. Prefix, eight
44. Midday
45. Hawaiian honeycreeper
46. Bristle
48. Tier
50. Small truck
51. Scottish river

puzzle 67

ACROSS
1. Pet form of Leonard
4. Naive person
8. Beak
11. Black
13. Earthen pot
14. Legendary emperor of China
15. Off-Broadway theater award
16. Humility
18. Cleaning lady
20. Consumed
21. Surgical saw
23. Fire remains
24. - up, excited
25. Narcotics agent
27. Boss on a shield
31. To
33. Monetary unit of Romania
34. Chief
35. Apparently successful project
36. Mother of Apollo
38. Black
39. Some
41. Prefix, intestine
43. Roman general
46. Door handles
47. Having original purity
49. Small particle
52. Mature
53. Beats by tennis service
54. Mature
55. Japanese currency
56. Dregs
57. Prefix, whale

DOWN
1. Zodiac sign
2. Wane
3. Boned cutlet
4. In name only
5. To the sheltered side
6. Island (France)
7. Feigns
8. Russian no
9. Relax
10. Boatswain
12. Lowest high tide
17. Book of the Bible
19. Level of karate proficiency
21. Brutal gangster
22. U.S. divorce city
23. Acuity
26. Female ruff
28. Imposing
29. Coffin stand
30. Upon
32. Verbal exams
37. Yoko -
40. Of birth
42. Type of automatic gear selector (1-3)
43. Desex female dog
44. Incite
45. Charge over property
46. Leg joint
48. Freeze
50. Open
51. Greeted

puzzle 68

ACROSS
1. Sunbeam
4. Clump of trees
8. Nocturnal bird
11. Iridescent gem
13. 6th month of the Jewish calendar
14. Hive insect
15. Abominable snowman
16. Bequests
18. Anigh
20. Takes a quick look at
21. Milk and egg drink
23. Hallucinogenic drug
24. Cheer
25. Naked
27. Taj Mahal site
31. Officiating priest of a mosque
33. Work unit
34. Wreck
35. Hawaiian goose
36. Russian no
38. Newt
39. Exclamation of surprise
41. Sickness of stomach
43. Glowed
46. Paradises
47. Lace scarf
49. Prehistoric sepulchral tomb
52. Last month
53. Scorch
54. Unique thing
55. Prefix, the earth
56. Wee
57. Merry

DOWN
1. - Rene. Mo
2. Primate
3. Turkish sword
4. Spanish dance
5. River in central Europe
6. Label
7. Snares
8. Off-Broadway theater award
9. Seven days
10. Minus
12. Waterfall
17. Timber tree
19. An age
21. Ireland
22. Brave
23. Pertaining to a legend
26. Arid
28. Surmising
29. Prevalent
30. Rectangular pier
32. Intended
37. - kwon do (Korean martial art)
40. Robbery
42. Remarkable
43. Complacent
44. Robust
45. Upon
46. Dash
48. Garland
50. Large body of water
51. Attempt

puzzle 69

ACROSS
1. Speck
4. Be foolishly fond of
8. Road surfacing
11. In bed
13. Enough
14. Room within a harem
15. Pen
16. Pertaining to meteors
18. Sacrificial bench
20. Full of ruts
21. Victualer
23. Superlative suffix
24. Yoko -
25. Colour of unbleached linen
27. Genuine
31. Intentions
33. Atmosphere
34. Jealousy
35. Egyptian deity
36. Type of automatic gear selector (1-3)
38. Rocky peak
39. Freeze
41. Salt solution
43. The Hindu Destroyer
46. Downy duck
47. Skin tumor
49. Long fish
52. Vex
53. Ireland
54. Pierce with knife
55. An infusion
56. Hardens
57. Affirmative response

DOWN
1. Skilled
2. Japanese sash
3. Tumor
4. Mark out boundaries of
5. Unique thing
6. Young child
7. Pitchers
8. Misdeed
9. Entrance
10. Risque
12. Girl's plaything
17. Bizarre
19. Golf peg
21. Bath requisite
22. Military detachment
23. People of European/Asian derivation
26. Chest bone
28. Completeness
29. Shakespeare's river
30. Harp-like instrument
32. The Hindu Destroyer
37. Radiation unit
40. Walking sticks
42. Dregs
43. Struck
44. In this place
45. Every
46. Send out
48. Crude mineral
50. New Guinea seaport
51. Ethnic telecaster

puzzle 70

ACROSS
1. Metal can
4. American state
8. Firearm
11. Poems
13. Pleasing
14. Before
15. Cleanse
16. Sentiments
18. Swollen
20. Beginning
21. Nut variety
23. Dined
24. Japanese sash
25. Chew on a bone
27. Scheme
31. Tear
33. An age
34. Beancurd
35. Brink
36. Yugoslavian
38. Forefront
39. My, French (Plural)
41. Downy ducks
43. Bulb vegetable
46. Barracouta
47. Beat severely
49. Scorning person
52. Cut off
53. Prompts
54. Serbian folk dance
55. Donkey
56. Decades
57. An infusion

DOWN
1. Haul
2. Highest mountain in Crete
3. Very young bird
4. Inaptitude
5. Bound
6. Top card
7. Spartan serf
8. Clan
9. Incite
10. Nidus
12. Avoid
17. Inappropriate
19. Drinking vessel
21. Eroded
22. In bed
23. Consciousness
26. Land measure
28. Ribbon emblematic of love
29. Distant
30. Cloistered women
32. Disband troops
37. Prefix, life
40. Make law
42. Writing table
43. Earthen pot
44. Temple
45. Little devils
46. Submachine gun
48. Take to court
50. Bullfight call
51. Large snake

puzzle 71

ACROSS
1. Peak
4. Distant
8. Congeal
11. Prefix, dry
13. Fiddling Roman emperor
14. Room within a harem
15. Dutch cheese
16. Defective pronunciation
18. Mark of omission
20. Styles
21. Cricket sundries
23. Pressure symbol
24. Prefix, three
25. Egyptian deity
27. Person in authority
31. Small nail
33. Exclamation of surprise
34. Coal dust
35. Looker
36. South African currency
38. Female deer
39. Egos
41. Transvestism
43. Climb
46. Spirit
47. Cultivated cabbage
49. An evil
52. Revised form of Esperanto
53. Political combine
54. Soon
55. Time of sunshine
56. Desires
57. Deity

DOWN
1. Chop
2. Captained
3. Custom
4. Forebears
5. Exploit
6. Part of a circle
7. House parts
8. Benevolent
9. Brink
10. Puts down
12. - Khayyam
17. Hips
19. Knock with knuckles
21. Suffix, diminutive
22. Photograph of bones (1-3)
23. Study of speech sounds
26. Exclamation of surprise
28. Treating with iodine
29. Jeers
30. Stalk
32. Small crustaceans eaten by whales
37. Scale note
40. Horse race
42. Exploding star
43. Slide
44. Musical ending
45. Nautical call
46. Black
48. Beer
50. Dove's call
51. Finish

puzzle 72

ACROSS
1. Drinking vessel
4. Songbird
8. Open
11. Once again
13. Prefix, sun
14. Humour
15. Pen
16. Person's individual speech pattern
18. Packs fully
20. Murder by suffocation
21. Purgative injections
23. Monetary unit of Japan
24. Colorful form of the common carp
25. Rube
27. Beaten by tennis service
31. Roof overhang
33. - Guevara
34. Hindu music
35. Outbuilding
36. Assistant
38. Singer, - "King" Cole
39. Conger
41. Battle fleet
43. Slope
46. Grass trimming tool
47. Ate
49. Stead
52. Talent
53. Girl's plaything
54. Rip
55. Change colour of
56. Relax
57. Underwater craft

DOWN
1. Taxi
2. Prefix, one
3. See
4. Capricious
5. Clarets
6. Biblical high priest
7. Zeus changed her to stone
8. One who is indebted
9. Select
10. Suffix, diminutive
12. Annelid
17. Of the moon
19. Exclamation of surprise
21. Supplements
22. Ark builder
23. Hasty flight
26. Greek letter
28. Pet birds
29. Minor oath
30. Information
32. Paradises
37. Work unit
40. Musical study piece
42. Thaw
43. Great quantity
44. Lorikeet
45. Poker stake
46. Long fish
48. New Zealand bird
50. French, water
51. An urban area

puzzle 73

ACROSS
1. Infant's protective garment
4. Ova
8. Mine
11. River in central Europe
13. Photograph of bones (1-3)
14. Small truck
15. Prefix, foreign
16. Produced from petroleum
18. Given to joking
20. Erse
21. Bored out
23. Resinous deposit
24. Intention
25. East Indies palm
27. Small particle
31. Network
33. Moose
34. Wise
35. Knee
36. Russian no
38. Female ruff
39. Prefix, whale
41. Combined resources
43. Spread
46. Major artery
47. Channel leading away
49. A particular
52. Dined
53. Is not
54. Attention
55. Cot
56. Supplements
57. Vietnam

DOWN
1. Crate
2. Carp-like fish
3. One of the tribes of Israel
4. Means to an end
5. Hoar
6. Gun (Slang)
7. Its capital is Damascus
8. Hungarian sheepdog
9. Inflammation (Suffix)
10. Technical college (Colloq)
12. Space
17. Killer whales
19. Knowledge
21. Sturdy wool fiber
22. Ireland
23. Wordsworth, Coleridge, and Southey (4.5)
26. 3 Thickness
28. Muslin
29. Double curve
30. Reward
32. Of a Duke
37. Rocky peak
40. Eagle's nest
42. Auricular
43. Pierce with knife
44. Meat paste
45. Prevaricated
46. Adolescent pimples
48. Question
50. An age
51. 13th letter of the Hebrew alphabet

puzzle 74

ACROSS
1. Fly larva
4. Absent
8. Prefix, foot
11. On top of
13. Glass panel
14. Beer
15. Fiddling Roman emperor
16. Contender in the Olympic Games
18. Moon age at start of year
20. Works for
21. Abalone (3.3)
23. Finish
24. Sum
25. Tree frog
27. Group of two
31. Frozen precipitation
33. Normal
34. American university
35. Fleet rodent
36. 8th letter of the Hebrew alphabet
38. Fish eggs
39. Mount - , N.W. Qld. mining town
41. Hamper
43. Blockade
46. Nerd
47. Throne of a bishop
49. Assistant
52. In the past
53. Jetty
54. Threesome
55. French, good
56. Raced
57. Lair

DOWN
1. Bread roll
2. Open
3. Bullfighter
4. Religious writings
5. - Disney
6. Some
7. Arab country
8. Duo
9. Dash
10. Lairs
12. No (Colloq)
17. Rice field
19. Exclamation of surprise
21. Broad ribbon
22. Dame - Everage, Humphries' character
23. Toward the earth
26. New Guinea seaport
28. Convict
29. Agave
30. Antlered beast
32. Find weight of
37. Hasten
40. Oozes
42. Tidy
43. Strike breaker
44. The villain in Othello
45. English college
46. Endure
48. Briefly immerse in water
50. Expire
51. An age

puzzle 75

ACROSS
1. French vineyard
4. Person in authority
8. Last month
11. Female relative
13. Capital of Yemen
14. - de Janeiro
15. Erode
16. Illuminate
18. Wash out
20. Rears
21. Tenets
23. Egyptian serpent
24. French, water
25. Relax
27. One of the Disciples
31. Head cook
33. And not
34. Sicilian volcano
35. African antelope
36. Hew
38. Greek goddess of the dawn
39. That woman
41. Of delicate beauty
43. Bass singer
46. Wens
47. The heavens
49. Hawaiian honeycreeper
52. Atomic mass unit
53. An appointment
54. European race
55. Fox
56. Greek god of love
57. Pig enclosure

DOWN
1. Crow call
2. Regret
3. Undisputed
4. Birth
5. Lazy
6. Unit of loudness
7. Ignores
8. Of urine
9. Nexus
10. Pedal digits
12. Decorate (Xmas tree)
17. Tree
19. Not
21. Ship's floor
22. Island of Hawaii
23. Heavier-than-air craft
26. Scale note
28. Kitchen implements
29. Nautical mile
30. Simple
32. Hard to please
37. Dance step
40. Multitude
42. Inflammation (Suffix)
43. Vanquish
44. Ammunition (Colloq)
45. Potato (Colloq)
46. Roman censor
48. Otic organ
50. Buddhist temple
51. Climbing plant

puzzle 76

ACROSS
1. Maize protein
5. Jab
9. Japanese currency
12. Leer
13. Mysterious symbol
14. Dined
15. Double curve
16. Holly
17. Groove
18. Apportion
20. Capital of Tunisia
22. Full of regret
25. Brown-capped boletus mushroom
26. Contribution to discussion
27. Prefix, over
28. Monetary unit of Romania
31. Short take-off and landing aircraft
32. Negating word
33. Circuits
34. Greek goddess of the dawn
35. Strike
36. Fathers
37. Fairy queen
38. Lose one's way
39. Belly button
42. Well ventilated
43. Biblical high priest
44. Cuts off
46. Pig meat
50. Everything
51. A Great Lake
52. Agave
53. Cereal
54. Long period of time
55. Moist with dew

DOWN
1. Menagerie
2. Ovum
3. Island (France)
4. Necessary
5. Pelletize
6. Govern
7. Monad
8. The right side
9. Story
10. Sewing case
11. Devices for fishing
19. Not at home
21. Toward the top
22. Stand
23. To
24. Epic poetry
25. Sever
27. Drunkard
28. Fat
29. Fencing sword
30. Former Soviet Union
32. Pen point
33. Floating leaf
35. English astronomer
36. Knight's title
37. Objective case of I
38. More sensible
39. Close to
40. Friend
41. Evil
42. Capital of Western Samoa
45. Crude mineral
47. Bullfight call
48. Tier
49. Unlocking implement

puzzle 77

ACROSS
1. Ran from
5. Lichen
9. Mineral spring
12. Simple
13. Capital of Western Samoa
14. Nipple
15. Abominable snowman
16. Delivery vehicles
17. Mature
18. Metal spike
20. Fleet rodents
22. Scottish pudding
25. Overact
26. Coral island
27. Purchase
28. Assist
31. Member of the Conservative Party
32. Cheer
33. Floor covering
34. Secret agent
35. British, a fool
36. African tribe
37. Weir
38. Persian musical instrument
39. Abode of the dead
42. Female relative
43. Conger
44. Booth
46. 3 Weapons
50. An age
51. Angered
52. Russian no
53. Soldiers
54. Yield
55. Ethereal

DOWN
1. Doomed
2. New Guinea seaport
3. Superlative suffix
4. Deathly
5. Song thrush
6. Iridescent gem
7. Transgress
8. Walk nonchalantly
9. Mast
10. Book leaf
11. Primates
19. Sicken
21. Part of the verb "to be"
22. Headwear
23. At the apex
24. Bloody
25. Questioning exclamation
27. Flying mammal
28. Isn't
29. Monetary unit of Peru
30. Gloomy
32. Edge
33. Troublesome tropical plant grown for hedges and flowers
35. Characteristically French
36. Prohibit
37. Perform
38. Soft leather
39. Appear
40. In this place
41. Dash
42. Old
45. Crude mineral
47. Cereal
48. Sea (French)
49. Pig enclosure

puzzle 78

ACROSS
1. Implement
5. Punch
9. Taxi
12. Land measure
13. Vex
14. Anger
15. Large almost tailless rodent
16. Askew
17. Spread out for drying
18. Exclamation of acclaim
20. Ostrich-like birds
22. Japanese form of self-defense
25. Colorful form of the common carp
26. Graceful birds
27. Spanish hero
28. Gymnasium
31. High, clear ringing sound
32. Fox
33. American Indian
34. Mount - , N.W. Qld. mining town
35. Yelp
36. Shall (Archaic)
37. Become firm
38. Capable of being done
39. Chocolate powder
42. Prefix, foreign
43. Expression of disgust
44. Title
46. Labels
50. Biblical high priest
51. Dutch cheese
52. Hip bones
53. Lair
54. Make temporary sleeping place (Colloq)
55. Monetary unit

DOWN
1. Faucet
2. Wood sorrel
3. Killer whale
4. Food scrap
5. Applause
6. U.S. State
7. An evergreen
8. Fishing rod
9. Quote
10. Region
11. Cots
19. Egos
21. Hello there
22. Italian wine province
23. Certainly
24. Japanese syllabic script
25. Young goat
27. Policeman
28. Clutch
29. Shout
30. Measure out
32. Make lace
33. Disordered
35. Lambed
36. Male offspring
37. Therefore
38. Considers
39. Prompted
40. Leer
41. Facial feature
42. Christmas
45. Fuss
47. Beer
48. Garbage can
49. Took a seat

puzzle 79

ACROSS
1. Chances
5. Iridescent gem
9. Hold up
12. Verse
13. Glass panel
14. An age
15. Withered
16. Heroic
17. Play division
18. Indian currency
20. Greek goddesses of the seasons
22. Indian city
25. Marsh
26. Concur
27. Battle
28. Needlefish
31. Peruse
32. Prefix, not
33. At the bow of a vessel
34. Work unit
35. Sack
36. Infants
37. Domestic pet
38. Extravagant
39. Church council
42. The villain in Othello
43. New Zealand parrot
44. Is not
46. Marsh plant
50. Otic organ
51. Positions
52. Suffix, diminutive
53. Snoop
54. Monetary unit of China
55. Fresh-water fish

DOWN
1. Operations (colloq)
2. Female deer
3. The (German)
4. Daubed
5. Unseals
6. Father
7. Black bird
8. Lustful male
9. Back
10. Killer whale
11. Restrain
19. Not
21. Not off
22. Female horse
23. Maturing agent
24. Haul
25. Avid admirer
27. Flu (Colloq)
28. Mongolian desert
29. Greek god of war
30. 20th letter of the Hebrew alphabet
32. Henpeck
33. Privileged
35. Corporal
36. Sack
37. Perform
38. Roman
39. Beehive
40. Long period of time
41. Never
42. Ancient Peruvian
45. Former coin of France
47. Greek letter
48. Etcetera
49. Scottish river

puzzle 80

ACROSS
1. Praise
5. Root vegetable
9. Jack in cribbage
12. Region
13. Spool
14. The self
15. Turkish governors
16. Arm bone
17. An infusion
18. Sweet potatoes
20. Light beam
22. Austrian river
25. French, good
26. Grey
27. Resinous deposit
28. Become firm
31. Poker stake
32. Legume
33. Uncommon
34. Zodiac sign
35. Spread out for drying
36. Eagle's nest
37. Sack
38. Whirlpools
39. Chirp
42. Crocodile (Colloq)
43. Lubricant
44. Reverberate
46. Large trees
50. Eggs
51. Incursion
52. Once again
53. Female swan
54. Stable attendant
55. Wee

DOWN
1. Laboratory
2. Land measure
3. U-turn (Colloq)
4. Carnivorous marsupial
5. Mist
6. Long fish
7. Even (poet.)
8. Aztec god of rain
9. Devices for fishing
10. Double curve
11. Hog
19. To endure
21. Prefix meaning without
22. Indian pulses
23. First class (1-3)
24. Western pact
25. Bleat
27. Captained
28. Hindu garment
29. A Great Lake
30. Golf mounds
32. Wooden pin
33. Historically, a British soldier
35. Becomes narrow
36. Fuss
37. To exist
38. Wear away
39. Fowl enclosure
40. Bee nest
41. Dash
42. Stylish
45. Coral island
47. Black bird
48. Knowledge
49. Two-up

puzzle 81

ACROSS
1. Helsinki citizen
5. Tree frog
9. Mineral spring
12. To the sheltered side
13. Portent
14. Lavatory (Colloq)
15. Network of nerves
16. Hog sound
17. Top card
18. Antlered beast
20. Inamorato
22. Bell tower
25. Lair
26. Smell
27. Affirmative response
28. Marsh
31. Genuine
32. Female ruff
33. At the bow of a vessel
34. Finish
35. Beetle
36. Fountain
37. Skilled
38. Small tower
39. The elbow
42. Charged particles
43. Former coin of France
44. Current month
46. Colour of unbleached linen
50. Superlative suffix
51. Bargain event
52. Word used in comparisons
53. Affirmative vote
54. Obey
55. Hawaiian honeycreeper

DOWN
1. Distant
2. Island (France)
3. Seine
4. Necessary
5. Bunk
6. Primordial giant in Norse myth
7. Pet form of Leonard
8. Leg joints
9. European race
10. Step
11. Vow
19. Go wrong
21. Not off
22. Drill
23. Paradise
24. A burden
25. Scottish river
27. Your (Colloq)
28. Tetrad
29. Sea eagle
30. After deductions
32. Hold up
33. Norse god
35. Of Denmark
36. Amusement
37. Perform
38. Carried
39. At sea
40. Inquisitive
41. Strangely attractive
42. Small island
45. Not
47. Greek letter
48. Uncooked
49. Prefix, one

puzzle 82

ACROSS
1. Tailless cat
5. Diving bird
9. Father
12. Region
13. Remarkable
14. Room within a harem
15. English college
16. Hawaiian feast
17. Israeli submachine gun
18. Hints
20. Bird prisons
22. Volcanic material
25. Electrical resistance unit
26. Eagle's nest
27. Lad
28. Little devil
31. Crocodile (Colloq)
32. Money (Slang)
33. Prayer
34. Possessed
35. Two
36. Person born under the sign of the Ram
37. Prohibit
38. Fly an aircraft
39. Become narrow
42. Double curve
43. Monad
44. Zest
46. Rice wine
50. Tier
51. The maple
52. New Guinea currency unit
53. Abstract being
54. Fiddling Roman emperor
55. Card game

DOWN
1. Actress, - West
2. Talent
3. Prefix, new
4. Having a yellowish color
5. Guilt
6. Responsibility
7. Wood sorrel
8. Controversial
9. Cricketer, - Walters
10. Hoe-shaped axe
11. Speaking platform
19. Anger
21. Part of the verb "to be"
22. Technical college (Colloq)
23. Jaguarundi
24. Jab
25. Money (Slang)
27. Large snake
28. Hip bones
29. Flesh
30. Glass panel
32. Possess
33. Clergymen
35. Man of superior strength
36. Greeting
37. To exist
38. Aggression (Colloq)
39. Ripped
40. Soon
41. Church benches
42. Unique thing
45. Freeze
47. Very good (1-2)
48. New Zealand parrot
49. Consume

puzzle 83

ACROSS
1. Vases
5. Type of automatic gear selector (1-3)
9. Feline
12. Cry-baby
13. Prefix, air
14. Scottish expression
15. Swedish pop-group of the '70s
16. Rough earthenware
17. Falsehood
18. Old form or you or your
20. Chum
22. Ged gems
25. Peak
26. Spy
27. Mature
28. Sever
31. Pennant
32. To and -
33. Mast
34. Island of Denmark
35. Pep
36. Gleam
37. Minor admonishment
38. Coronets
39. Iodine solution
42. Ireland
43. Two
44. Terse
46. Freshwater duck
50. Even (poet.)
51. Indigo
52. Leer
53. Missus
54. Number of Muses
55. Musical symbol

DOWN
1. America (Abbr)
2. Hold up
3. Jack in cribbage
4. Performing on ice
5. Polynesian edible roots
6. Sweetheart
7. Noah's vessel
8. Russian money
9. Chill
10. Etching fluid
11. People in general
19. - up, excited
21. Toward the top
22. Rabble
23. Unattractive
24. A legume
25. In the past
27. Limb
28. Coconut husk fibre
29. Arm bone
30. Golf mounds
32. Spasm
33. Four-wheeled carriage
35. Roman god of fire
36. Knight's title
37. In the direction of
38. Name
39. A particular
40. One who is indebted
41. Levels of karate proficiency
42. Ireland
45. Prefix, one
47. The self
48. High-pitched
49. Sheltered side

puzzle 84

ACROSS
1. Small rodents
5. Reposed
9. An explosive
12. Scheme
13. Capable
14. Hasten
15. Garment edges
16. Every
17. Beer
18. Never
20. Cut wood
22. Craven person
25. Garbage can
26. Nautical, to the left
27. Lubricant
28. Large body of water
31. Cabbagelike plant
32. Skilled
33. Morning
34. Antiquity
35. Prefix, over
36. Brief halt
37. "The Raven" author
38. Whimbrel
39. Garden pest
42. As well as
43. An age
44. Brink
46. Town crier's call
50. Superlative suffix
51. Italian currency
52. Title
53. Female ruff
54. Lamb
55. Avoid

DOWN
1. Miles per hour
2. Island (France)
3. Eccentric wheel
4. Entrap
5. Scottish lord
6. Skilfully
7. Family
8. Clockwise
9. Melt
10. African river
11. - off, began golf game
19. Talent
21. Prefix meaning without
22. Shaped mass of food
23. Iridescent gem
24. A plain
25. Infant's protective garment
27. Paddle
28. Inner spirit
29. Gaelic
30. Once again
32. Owing
33. Leaves stranded
35. Exclusively
36. Purulence
37. The ratio between circumference and diameter
38. Wash
39. Prophet
40. Proboscis
41. Poker stake
42. Taj Mahal site
45. Expire
47. Exclamation of disgust
48. Australian bird
49. Buddhist sect

puzzle 85

ACROSS
1. Greet
5. Cleanse
9. Witness
12. Angers
13. Long walk
14. A delay
15. Death rattle
16. Entrance
17. Eggs
18. Sailors
20. Solidly fix in surrounding mass
22. An Australian
25. Crude mineral
26. Chose
27. Cattle low
28. Teenage lout
31. Commonsense
32. Clumsy person
33. Hip
34. Finish
35. Atmosphere
36. Storms
37. Shoemaker's tool
38. Violet antiseptic
39. Make ashamed
42. Ancient Peruvian
43. Flu (Colloq)
44. Charged particles
46. Override
50. Land measure
51. Tarn
52. Dash
53. Your (Colloq)
54. Former
55. Travel on

DOWN
1. Russian community
2. An age
3. Conger
4. Sleeping sickness flies
5. Maori hut
6. Helps
7. Snow runner
8. Heterosexual (Colloq)
9. Untidy person
10. Roof overhang
11. Minor oath
19. Assist
21. Objective case of I
22. First class (1-3)
23. On top of
24. Breeding horse
25. Money (Slang)
27. Spoil
28. Practitioner of yoga
29. Beasts of burden
30. Bottom
32. Lubricant
33. Corpse
35. For a short time
36. Fabulous bird
37. Similar to
38. Piece put in
39. Absent
40. Drill
41. Maturing agent
42. Writing fluids
45. Paddle
47. Biblical high priest
48. Small amount
49. Monad

puzzle 86

ACROSS
1. Pack fully
5. New Zealand parrot
9. Belonging to him
12. Subtle emanation
13. Cain's victim
14. Beer
15. 2nd letter of the Hebrew alphabet
16. Arm bone
17. Acne pimple
18. Panel
20. Ostrich-like birds
22. Eight tentacled creatures
25. Take to court
26. Valleys
27. City in NW Iran
28. Missus
31. Phoned
32. Young bear
33. Dirt
34. Printer's measures
35. Bleat
36. Cathedral
37. Chop
38. Subdebutante
39. Tartan
42. Springing gait
43. Sicken
44. Portable ice-box
46. Enough
50. Fold
51. Ululate
52. Roof overhang
53. Bitter vetch
54. A few
55. Tidy

DOWN
1. Taxi
2. Regret
3. Talent
4. Chinese game
5. New Zealand evergreen tree
6. Skilfully
7. Knowledge
8. Warning bell
9. Obscurity
10. Hip bones
11. Hardens
19. Raises
21. Masculine pronoun
22. Monster
23. Large mollusc
24. Decades
25. Weep
27. As
28. Atmosphere
29. Hoarfrost
30. Untidy person
32. Crow call
33. Person approaching the teens
35. Covers with dew
36. Twosome
37. Hello there
38. Manner
39. Wan
40. Fibber
41. Peaks
42. Glide on surface
45. Cracker biscuit
47. Not
48. Eggs
49. Soak

puzzle 87

ACROSS
1. Ululate
5. Russian emperor
9. Miles per hour
12. Greasy
13. Australian super-model
14. Beer
15. Portent
16. Death rattle
17. Thrash
18. Temporary settlement
20. Weaves wool
22. Antics
25. Prefix, the earth
26. Leave of absence
27. Evil
28. Farewell
31. Waterfall
32. Synthetic yttrium aluminum garnet
33. Metal spike
34. Hallucinogenic drug
35. Prohibit
36. Tugs
37. Sticky stuff
38. Old Scottish bullion coin
39. Nide
42. Ethereal
43. Of us
44. Notion
46. Candid
50. To endure
51. Booty
52. Hindu music
53. Gender
54. Desires
55. Door handle

DOWN
1. Court
2. Intention
3. Island (France)
4. Sharp-sighted
5. Expressions
6. Hit with hand
7. Everything
8. Smelled foul
9. Republic in W Africa
10. Plot of ground
11. Garment edges
19. Talent
21. Negative vote
22. Prison room
23. Line of revolution
24. Hang
25. To silence
27. Prohibit
28. Point of hook
29. Argument
30. Otherwise
32. Legendary emperor of China
33. The *Big Apple* (3,4)
35. Corporal
36. Jolt
37. Depart
38. Vanquishes
39. Large snakes
40. Hick
41. Large African antelope
42. Great age
45. Female deer
47. Kitchen utensil
48. The self
49. Arrest

puzzle 88

ACROSS
1. Pare
5. Growl
9. Annihilate
12. Narrow country road
13. Jot
14. First woman
15. Desires
16. Printer's mark, keep
17. Hive insect
18. Hour
20. Inter ashes
22. Short jacket
25. Yoko -
26. Worship
27. Large
28. Top card
31. Scottish hills
32. The sun
33. Tribe
34. Land measure
35. Hawaiian acacia
36. Haughty
37. Large barrel
38. Trundles
39. French claret
42. Opera solo
43. Optic organ
44. Bee nest
46. Switchblade
50. Part of a circle
51. Level
52. Relax
53. An infusion
54. Scottish headland
55. Cupola

DOWN
1. Wily
2. Not
3. Tavern
4. Harasses
5. Gadget
6. Musical symbol
7. Dined
8. Unranked seaman
9. Indian ox
10. Vow
11. Hammer head
19. Anger
21. Negative vote
22. Small yeast cake
23. River in central Europe
24. Solitary
25. Lubricant
27. Large snake
28. Agave
29. Hood-like membrane
30. Finishes
32. Male offspring
33. Wrinkled
35. Yeast-raised coffeecake
36. Greek letter
37. In the direction of
38. Songbirds
39. Flesh
40. Australian explorer
41. Prefix, ten
42. Birds
45. I have
47. Monetary unit of Vietnam
48. Doctrine
49. Victory sign

puzzle 89

ACROSS
1. A cross
5. Sacred Egyptian bird
9. Meadow
12. Sharpen
13. Raise
14. Sick
15. Islamic chieftain
16. Information
17. Owing
18. Toward the mouth
20. Wild Asian dog
22. Pickled
25. Mature
26. Ghastly
27. Prompt
28. Monetary unit of Japan
31. Food scraps
32. Diving bird
33. Roof overhang
34. Pressure symbol
35. Taxi
36. Keen
37. Exclamation of surprise
38. Leave high and dry
39. Rift
42. Ornamental brooch
43. Lubricant
44. Daring
46. Curved entrance
50. Revised form of Esperanto
51. Finishes
52. Ostrich-like bird
53. A charge
54. Blushing
55. In -, in all

DOWN
1. - Guevara
2. Gipsy lad
3. Prefix, one
4. Abnormal dryness of the skin
5. Homer's epic
6. Tie
7. If and only if
8. Gorge
9. Public swimming pool
10. 12th month of the Jewish calendar
11. To the sheltered side
19. Colour
21. Masculine pronoun
22. Splash
23. Yours and mine
24. Upper respiratory tract infection
25. Diving bird
27. Young bear
28. Heroic story
29. Level
30. Dweeb
32. Exclamation of surprise
33. US aviatrix, Amelia -
35. Slight arch
36. Etcetera
37. Similar to
38. Resembling suds
39. Skullcap
40. Conceal
41. Agave
42. One's parents (Colloq)
45. Yoko -
47. 17th letter of the Greek alphabet
48. Prefix, whale
49. Monetary unit of Vietnam

puzzle 90

ACROSS
1. Pome
5. Gael
9. Stitch
12. Prefix, air
13. Hautboy
14. Greek letter
15. Prayer
16. Swedish pop-group of the '70s
17. Flee
18. Felines
20. Biblical measure
22. Queen of Ahasuerus
25. Young dog
26. Master of ceremonies
27. Mouth part
28. British rule in India
31. Oceans
32. Female deer
33. Wallaroo
34. An explosive
35. Beldam
36. Effeminate male
37. Skilled
38. Like a marsh
39. Iodine solution
42. Rackets
43. Timid
44. Puts down
46. Drape
50. Falsehood
51. Minor oath
52. Off-Broadway theater award
53. Greek goddess of the dawn
54. - Ono
55. Variety

DOWN
1. Nipple
2. Conger
3. Land measure
4. Cockroaches (Colloq)
5. Raccoonlike carnivore
6. Wanes
7. Throw lightly
8. Item in a tea service
9. Yugoslavian
10. Sewing case
11. Desire
19. Dined
21. Toward the top
22. Waistcoat
23. Prayer ending
24. Shoo
25. Pastry item
27. Large tree remnant
28. Cricket scores
29. Curved entrance
30. Young kangaroo
32. Skilled
33. Range of hearing
35. English astronomer
36. Grandmother
37. Perform
38. Botch
39. Small island
40. U.S. State
41. Stains
42. Aborigine of Borneo
45. In the past
47. To endure
48. Pinch
49. Horse command

puzzle 91

ACROSS
1. Foolish
5. One pound sterling
9. Ethnic telecaster
12. A Great Lake
13. Official language of Pakistan
14. Garland
15. Tear
16. Great age
17. Last month
18. Every
20. Menu
22. Playful
25. Decade
26. Audibly
27. It is
28. Over there
31. Binds
32. Flying mammal
33. Musical ending
34. Rum
35. Sailor
36. Canadian province
37. Highest mountain in Crete
38. Photography requisite
39. Israeli orange
42. Thrashes
43. Carp-like fish
44. Lighting gas
46. Chopped
50. Vessel or duct
51. Card game
52. To the sheltered side
53. Printer's measures
54. Lotto-like gambling game
55. Broad

DOWN
1. The (German)
2. Land measure
3. Fish part
4. Monotonous
5. Tremble
6. Fertiliser
7. Revised form of Esperanto
8. Boneheads
9. Elide
10. Leather strap
11. Situate
19. Hallucinogenic drug
21. Prefix meaning without
22. Jet-assisted takeoff
23. Fetid
24. Student at mixed school
25. Small bird
27. Label
28. Pair of oxen
29. Scent
30. Grandmother
32. Large snake
33. Gratuity
35. Danzig
36. Sweet potato
37. Providing
38. Division of a long poem
39. Jitterbug
40. First man
41. Heraldry, wide horizontal stripe on shield
42. Advance money
45. Supplement existence
47. Biblical high priest
48. Marry
49. Born

puzzle 92

ACROSS
1. Having wings
5. Ship's company
9. Small cavity in a rock
12. Once existed
13. Possess
14. Mount - , N.W. Qld. mining town
15. Food
16. Old
17. Victory sign
18. Porous limestone
20. Knot
22. Lower in rank
25. Prefix, the earth
26. Abreast
27. Insane
28. Saturate
31. Stopper
32. To silence
33. Sicilian volcano
34. Superlative suffix
35. Public transport
36. Merrier
37. Total
38. Smallest
39. Australian political party
42. Large seaweed
43. An age
44. Consider
46. Statutes
50. Otic organ
51. Therefore
52. American state
53. Ethnic telecaster
54. Scottish headland
55. Hereditary factor

DOWN
1. Reverential fear
2. Meadow
3. Talent
4. Replenish
5. Abrade
6. Hindu music
7. First woman
8. Having the shape of a wedge
9. Exclamation of acclaim
10. Consumer
11. Erse
19. Small truck
21. Negative vote
22. Fresh-water fish
23. Epic poetry
24. Shopping centre
25. To silence
27. Mothers
28. Eye inflammation
29. Single items
30. Separate
32. Common eucalypt
33. Plug to keep out noise
35. Heavy load
36. Congeal
37. Therefore
38. Brief notes
39. Dregs
40. Semite
41. Prohibits
42. Beer barrels
45. Before
47. Dined
48. Ashen
49. That woman

puzzle 93

ACROSS
1. Cause to ring by striking
5. Monetary unit of Angola
9. Enemy
12. Region
13. Great age
14. Hallucinogenic drug
15. Ogle
16. Scottish headland
17. Island (France)
18. Summon
20. The elbow
22. Give to
25. Yoko -
26. Greek letter
27. New Guinea seaport
28. Scottish river
31. Challenge
32. Money (Slang)
33. Chaise
34. W.A. river
35. Machine for sending documents
36. Pursue
37. Large tree
38. Thwarted
39. Beatles' drummer, Ringo -
42. Hasty
43. Concealed
44. Water filled barricade
46. Variety
50. Prefix, one
51. Dame - Everage, Humphries' character
52. Enthusiasm
53. Seine
54. Train track
55. Upper respiratory tract infection

DOWN
1. Indian dish
2. Anger
3. Born
4. Trash
5. Cavalry spear
6. Seven days
7. Greek goddess of the dawn
8. Demented
9. French policeman
10. Capital of Norway
11. Paradise
19. Greek letter
21. Negative vote
22. Extinct bird
23. - Khayyam
24. Dweeb
25. Clumsy person
27. Brine-cured salmon
28. Indian pulses
29. Relax
30. Looked over
32. Large tree
33. Tibetan breed of small dog
35. Person who operates a farm
36. Long-leaved lettuce
37. Otherwise
38. Deadly
39. Avoid
40. Prong
41. Entrance
42. Indian queen
45. Room within a harem
47. Your (Colloq)
48. Dab
49. Biblical high priest

puzzle 94

ACROSS
1. Wife of Punch
5. Portico
9. A person
12. Military detachment
13. Vehicles
14. Otic organ
15. Hue
16. Finishes
17. Exclamation of surprise
18. Encircle
20. Loose fiber used for caulking
22. Pertaining to the Alps
25. Missus
26. Television repeat
27. Speck
28. Atomic mass unit
31. Side
32. Leg
33. Emperor of Russia
34. Firmament
35. 13th letter of the Hebrew alphabet
36. Pennants
37. Change colour of
38. The Muse of astronomy
39. Forbidden
42. Scorning person
43. Exclamation of surprise
44. Cooking implements
46. Time of prosperity
50. In favour of
51. Hip bones
52. Reverberate
53. Island of Denmark
54. Ethereal
55. Sloping walkway

DOWN
1. Protrude
2. Prefix, one
3. Racket
4. Rare metallic element
5. Vista
6. Sharp taste
7. W.A. river
8. Classify
9. Bill
10. Island of Hawaii
11. Small drink of liquor
19. Tavern
21. Similar to
22. Non-scientific studies
23. Welsh emblem
24. Make supplication
25. Mother (US)
27. Weir
28. Islamic call to prayer
29. The three wise men
30. Bear constellation
32. Horse command
33. Curdled milk
35. Nearsightedness
36. To and -
37. Perform
38. Retract
39. Dandy
40. Nautical call
41. Nee
42. Agitate
45. Bullfight call
47. Wood sorrel
48. Electrical resistance unit
49. Swab

puzzle 95

ACROSS
1. Indian ox
5. Network of nerves
9. A dynasty in China
12. Great age
13. Merit
14. Top card
15. Plan
16. Eager
17. An explosive
18. Assess
20. Make unhappy
22. King who couldn't hold back the tide
25. Garland
26. Wane
27. Once existed
28. Which person
31. Spurt forth
32. Hog
33. First son of Adam and Eve
34. Greek letter
35. Large tree remnant
36. Murder by suffocation
37. Top pupil
38. Breadwinner
39. Republic in W equatorial Africa
42. Slightly open
43. Bullfight call
44. Brave
46. Motor car
50. Scottish river
51. Executive Officer
52. Lowest high tide
53. Monetary unit of Japan
54. Dispatched
55. Variety

DOWN
1. Annihilate
2. Conger
3. Jeer
4. Lie
5. Consumed again
6. Roof overhang
7. Prefix, three
8. Invests
9. Headwear
10. Adolescent pimples
11. After deductions
19. Dined
21. The ratio between circumference and diameter
22. Bird prison
23. Adjoin
24. U.S. space agency
25. A delay
27. Hairpiece
28. Caution
29. Long walk
30. Unique thing
32. Plague
33. Seedless raisin
35. Thrusts forward
36. Bleat
37. Perform
38. Oust
39. Deities
40. To the sheltered side
41. "Has - ". Person who once was
42. Prayer ending
45. Chop
47. U-turn (Colloq)
48. Faucet
49. Open

puzzle 96

ACROSS
1. Pile
5. Toward the mouth
9. Worthless dog
12. Killer whale
13. Bay
14. Land measure
15. Abominable snowman
16. Fencing sword
17. Hallucinogenic drug
18. Chaise
20. Mothers
22. Nephew of King Arthur
25. Black
26. Hips
27. Bundle of money
28. Item of headwear
31. Unwrap
32. Eccentric wheel
33. Therefore
34. Golf peg
35. - and Yang
36. Egyptian capital
37. Soil
38. Consisting of herbs
39. Hake hazy
42. Expression used when accident happens
43. Otic organ
44. Upswept hairdo
46. Tramp
50. An age
51. Indian peasant
52. Unique thing
53. Wily
54. Sailors
55. Having pedal digits

DOWN
1. Bingo-like game
2. Before
3. Play division
4. Countryman
5. Large body of water
6. Resembling a rope
7. Greeting
8. Thought
9. Serene
10. Bear constellation
11. Clarets
19. Belonging to him
21. Near to
22. Surfeit
23. First class (1-3)
24. Broad
25. Fruit conserve
27. Ashen
28. Manger
29. Taj Mahal site
30. Pond
32. Spanish hero
33. Range of hearing
35. Curdled milk
36. Brown-capped boletus mushroom
37. Therefore
38. Loud derisory cries
39. Hive insects
40. Nobleman
41. Ravel
42. Scent
45. Monetary unit of Burma
47. Yoko -
48. Hive insect
49. W.A. river

puzzle 97

ACROSS
1. Pastry items
5. Reposed
9. Forefront
12. Colour of unbleached linen
13. Root of the taro
14. I have
15. Direct one's way
16. Waistcoat
17. Prefix, not
18. Prayer ending
20. Vapid
22. Pertaining to reign
25. Yoko -
26. Bitter
27. Hairpiece
28. Weep
31. Stylish
32. The sun
33. Amerce
34. An age
35. Owing
36. Filleted
37. Anger
38. Card game
39. Virtual
42. Converts to leather
43. Raises
44. Redact
46. Be defeated
50. Highest mountain in Crete
51. Rice wine
52. Fencing sword
53. Apex
54. One of two identical people
55. Stitched

DOWN
1. Church bench
2. Freeze
3. Sea eagle
4. Pertaining to the Sudan
5. Even
6. Capital of Yemen
7. Egos
8. Being foolishly fond of
9. Musical instrument of India
10. Shakespeare's river
11. Hawaiian goose
19. Insane
21. Negative vote
22. Sprint contest
23. Reverberate
24. Smile
25. Lubricant
27. Alas
28. Hyperbolic sine
29. Unique thing
30. English monk
32. Take to court
33. Sailors' forward cabins
35. Most parched
36. Bread roll
37. Part of the verb to be
38. Consumed
39. Stop
40. Upswept hairdo
41. As soon as possible
42. Maori image
45. Black bird
47. Open
48. Stitch
49. Even (poet.)

puzzle 98

ACROSS
1. Chain armour
5. Knave
9. Overact
12. Agave
13. Consumer
14. Bullfight call
15. Prefix, foreign
16. Information
17. Female ruff
18. Lowest high tide
20. Skill
22. Pertaining to Jews
25. Prefix, the earth
26. Spy
27. French, good
28. Your (Colloq)
31. Part played
32. Prefix, life
33. Jitterbug
34. Hallucinogenic drug
35. Japanese word of respect
36. Sulked
37. Legume
38. Stick together
39. Water wheel
42. Hired thug
43. Mature
44. Madam
46. Sand hill
50. Island (France)
51. Fencing sword
52. Iridescent gem
53. Captained
54. Close to
55. Glimpse

DOWN
1. Maximum
2. Beer
3. Charged particle
4. Lionlike
5. One of the 12 tribes of Israel
6. As soon as possible
7. Prefix, whale
8. Mythical sea monster
9. Israeli round dance
10. Smart - , show-off
11. Humble
19. Superlative suffix
21. Negative vote
22. Medieval Scandinavian chieftain
23. Personalities
24. Fuse together
25. Sticky stuff
27. Garbage can
28. Exclamation of fright
29. Always
30. Advise
32. Bleat
33. Average man
35. Sailors
36. Cattle low
37. The ratio between circumference and diameter
38. Arriver
39. Metal spike
40. Leer
41. Marsh plant
42. Greek goddess of the earth
45. Primate
47. Raises
48. Doze
49. Cathedral city

puzzle 99

ACROSS
1. Always
5. Couple
9. Television frequency
12. Prefix, part
13. Gaelic
14. Sunbeam
15. Mexican currency
16. Exclamations of surprise
17. Moose
18. Lofty
20. Abrade
22. Most mean
25. Before
26. Seize illegally
27. Pig enclosure
28. Tell on
31. Desires
32. Meadow
33. Melody
34. Japanese word of respect
35. New Zealand parrot
36. Rowed
37. Prefix, the earth
38. Bowers
39. Lure
42. Remarkable
43. Reverential fear
44. Pornography (Colloq)
46. Tear
50. Buddhist sect
51. As well as
52. Fencing sword
53. Superlative suffix
54. June 6, 1944
55. Ocean fluctuation

DOWN
1. Extrasensory perception
2. Victory sign
3. Printer's measures
4. People in rebellion
5. Distributed cards
6. European mountain range
7. Fire remains
8. Discover
9. Fertiliser
10. One of two equal parts
11. Bag-shaped fish trap
19. Egyptian serpent
21. Masculine pronoun
22. Purchases
23. At sea
24. E Indian shrub yielding hemp
25. Greek letter
27. Large body of water
28. Former coin of Spain
29. Unique thing
30. Cots
32. Zodiac sign
33. Stool
35. Panel of special keys
36. Killer whale
37. Depart
38. Bother
39. Stupefy
40. Female sheep
41. Monetary unit
42. Bear constellation
45. Aged
47. Prefix, over
48. - Kelly
49. Scottish river

puzzle 100

ACROSS
1. Baton
5. Type of automatic gear selector (1-3)
9. Prefix, whale
12. Fever
13. Hip bones
14. Bullfight call
15. Prefix, foreign
16. Narcotics agent
17. Actress, - West
18. Storm
20. Persian lords
22. Russian money
25. A charge
26. Improvise (speech)
27. Obtain
28. Law enforcement agency
31. Confined
32. Cot
33. Avid
34. An age
35. Sticky stuff
36. Fail
37. Bee product
38. Valleys
39. Nerd
42. Very dry champagne
43. Otic organ
44. Pen
46. Portent
50. The self
51. Reposed
52. American Indian
53. My, French (Plural)
54. U.S. TV award
55. Obey

DOWN
1. Bee product
2. Mature
3. Cloistered woman
4. Leave orbit
5. Tint
6. Blue-gray
7. Atmosphere
8. Din
9. Unconsciousness
10. Dash
11. Golf mounds
19. Long-sleeved linen vestment
21. Masculine pronoun
22. Take by force
23. River in central Europe
24. Arm bone
25. Gave food to
27. Prefix, the earth
28. Ongoing hostility
29. Prefix, well
30. Writing fluids
32. Crate
33. Casual gathering
35. Jabber
36. Influenza
37. Plural of I
38. Sleazy
39. Consider
40. Money paid for work
41. Greek god of love
42. Projecting edge
45. Braggart (Colloq) (1,2)
47. Anger
48. Horse command
49. - Kelly

solution 3

	I	T		J	E	W	E	L
I	S	O	L	A	T	E		I	N
N		P	I	T	A		O	N	O
A	N		D	O		A	R	C	
N	O	B				M	A	T	E
E	N	O	W			D	U	B	
	A	R	E		M	E		S	O
A	G	E		H	A	L	O		A
T	O		H	A	R	I	C	O	T
	N	E	E	D	S		A	N	

ACROSS
1. Neuter singular pronoun
3. Gem
7. Quarantine
9. Prefix meaning not
11. Middle Eastern bread
12. Yoko -
13. Prefix meaning without
15. Perform
16. Part of a circle
17. Jack in cribbage
19. Pal
21. Enough
23. Name
24. Land measure
25. Objective case of I
27. Therefore
28. Mature
29. Nimbus
31. In the direction of
32. Kidney bean
34. Necessities
35. Prefix meaning without

DOWN
1. Part of the verb to be
2. Apex
3. Jet-assisted takeoff
4. Greek letter
5. Plural of I
6. Soothing medicine
7. Vapid
8. Bottle top
10. Negative vote
12. Toward the mouth
14. Polygon having nine sides
16. Part of the verb "to be"
18. Drill
20. Torpedo vessel (1-4)
22. Plural of I
25. Red planet
26. Biblical high priest
28. Near to
29. Possessed
30. Wood sorrel
32. Masculine pronoun
33. Not off

solution 4

	I	N		E	B	O	N	Y	
P	S	A	L	T	E	R		O	N
L		B	A	T	E		F	R	O
O	F		V	E		I	L	K	
N	O	B				F	E	E	D
K	I	L	O				E	R	R
	B	I	N		B	E		S	O
A	L	P		S	E	L	F		I
M	E		H	A	L	I	B	U	T
		S	T	E	M	S		I	S

ACROSS
1. Prefix meaning not
3. Black wood
7. Psalmbook
9. Not off
11. Restrain
12. To and -
13. Belonging to
15. Plural of I
16. Family
17. ...ck in cribbage
19. ...e food to
21. ..., thousand
23. G... ong
24. Ga... e can
25. To e...
27. There...
28. Peak
29. Ego
31. Objective ...se of I
32. Flatfish
34. Stalks
35. Part of the verb to be

DOWN
1. Part of the verb to be
2. Arrest
3. Suffix, diminutive
4. Hive insect
5. Otherwise
6. Types of cricket deliveries
7. Fall heavily
8. Statute
10. Negative vote
12. Run from
14. Weaknesses
16. Providing
18. Radar screen element
20. Legal right
22. Not off
25. Units of loudness
26. Biblical high priest
28. Part of the verb "to be"
29. Uncle -, USA personified
30. Law enforcement agency
32. Masculine pronoun
33. Objective case of we

solution 5

	U	P		I	L	I	U	M	
T	S	E	T	S	E	S		I	N
A		P	U	L	E		A	D	O
G	O		B	E		P	E	D	
U	P	S				I	R	E	D
S	A	L	T				O	N	O
	C	O	O		A	S		S	O
H	I	P		P	A	I	L		M
I	T		A	S	H	R	A	M	S
	Y	E	T	I	S		W	E	

ACROSS
1. Toward the top
3. Hipbone
7. Sleeping sickness flies
9. Prefix meaning not
11. Whimper
12. Fuss
13. Depart
15. To exist
16. Prefix, foot
17. Raises
19. Angered
21. Seasoning
23. Yoko -
24. Dove's call
25. Similar to
27. Therefore
28. Coxa
29. Bucket
31. Neuter singular pronoun
32. Hindu religious retreats
34. Abominable snowmen
35. Plural of I

DOWN
1. Objective case of we
2. Energy
3. Small island
4. Sheltered side
5. Part of the verb to be
6. Refuse heaps
7. Spanish river
8. Vat
10. Negative vote
12. Prefix, air
14. The state of being opaque
16. The ratio between circumference and diameter
18. Splash
20. Ill-fates
22. In the direction of
25. Exclamations of surprise
26. Knight's title
28. Hello there
29. Pressure symbol
30. Statute
32. Near to
33. Objective case of I

solution 6

P	O	T			C	Z	A	R		M	E	S
E	V	E	N		H	A	S	H		I	L	K
R	A	C	Y		U	N	K	I	N	D	L	Y
		T	E	A	R	Y		N	O	I	S	E
E	X	O	T	I	C		C	O	S			
E	R	N		D	H	A	L		E	B	B	S
L	A	I	N		I	D	A		S	L	U	E
S	Y	C	E		L	O	S	E		A	C	T
			A	W	L		S	T	A	C	K	S
S	A	B	R	E		S	M	A	C	K		
C	A	E	S	A	R	E	A		M	O	T	T
A	R	E		N	E	A	T		E	U	R	O
B	E	N		S	E	R	E			T	I	E

ACROSS
1. Cooking implement
4. Emperor of Russia
8. My, French (Plural)
11. Level
13. Jumble
14. Family
15. Risque
16. Mean
18. Tearful
20. Sound
21. Foreign
23. Long-leaved lettuce
24. Sea eagle
25. Indian pulses
27. Wanes
31. Reclined
33. Highest mountain in Crete
34. Swing around
35. Stable attendant
36. Be defeated
38. Play division
39. Shoemaker's tool
41. Piles
43. Cavalry sword
46. Hit
47. Roman capital of Palestine
49. Clump of trees
52. Land measure
53. Tidy
54. Wallaroo
55. Scottish hill
56. Withered
57. Bind

DOWN
1. Each
2. Eggs
3. Constructive
4. British statesman
5. Whimsically comical
6. Question
7. Prefix, nose
8. Skirt coming to just below knee
9. Old cloth measures
10. Inner Hebrides island
12. Russian no
17. Nuzzles
19. Assist
21. Long fish
22. Photograph of bones (1-3)
23. School class member
26. Fuss
28. Total cut off of all light
29. Male of the deer
30. Hardens
32. Draws close to
37. Greek letter
40. Trains away from
42. Pinnacle
43. Strike breaker
44. River in central Switzerland
45. "Has - ". Person who once was
46. Scorch
48. Female ruff
50. Prefix, three
51. Pedal digit

solution 7

L	I	P		R	A	C	E		M	A	C
E	S	A	U		E	L	A	N		A	P	E
O	A	R	S		G	A	R	D	E	N	E	R
			A	E	G	I	S		E	V	A	D	E
D	U	M	D	U	M		I	D	E			
E	G	O		M	E	A	D		N	A	S	A
E	L	U	L		N	A	E		S	N	A	G
P	Y	R	E		T	H	O	R		I	L	E
			E	M	S		G	H	O	S	T	S
S	A	B	R	E		P	R	O	B	E		
C	A	E	S	A	R	E	A		I	T	C	H
A	R	E		N	E	A	P		E	T	U	I
B	E	N		S	E	T	H		E	R	S

ACROSS
1. Mouth part
4. Sprint contest
8. Raincoat
11. Son of Isaac and Rebekah
13. Dash
14. Primate
15. Paddles
16. Person who gardens
18. Sponsorship
20. Avoid
21. Hollow-nosed bullet
23. Carp-like fish
24. The self
25. Honey liquor
27. U.S. space agency
31. 12th month of the Jewish calendar
33. Not
34. Catch
35. Funeral fire
36. Norse god of thunder
38. Island (France)
39. Printer's measures
41. Spectres
43. Cavalry sword
46. Investigation
47. Roman capital of Palestine
49. Cause of scratching
52. Land measure
53. Lowest high tide
54. Sewing case
55. Scottish hill
56. Third son of Adam
57. Bitter vetch

DOWN
1. Zodiac sign
2. Mount - , N.W. Qld. mining town
3. Illicit lover
4. Military groups
5. Woe is me
6. Automobile
7. Finished
8. Supernatural power
9. Mimicked
10. Wax
12. Second-hand
17. Equalises
19. Common eucalypt
21. Profound
22. Unattractive
23. Ideogram
26. Exclamation of surprise
28. Aniseed liqueur
29. Seasoning
30. Matures
32. Ogles
37. 17th letter of the Greek alphabet
40. Income
42. Off-Broadway theater award
43. Strike breaker
44. River in central Switzerland
45. "Has - ". Person who once was
46. Bog fuel
48. Female ruff
50. Worthless dog
51. Belonging to him

solution 8

Z	E	E		R	I	S	E		S	O	L
O	R	T	S		E	B	B	S		A	C	E
O	G	E	E		D	E	S	S	E	R	T	S
		R	A	D	I	X		A	D	I	O	S
D	U	N	L	I	N		E	Y	E			
E	P	I		E	G	G	S		M	I	C	A
C	O	Z	Y		O	A	T		A	N	E	W
K	N	E	E		T	R	A	D		A	L	E
		T	A	E		B	E	A	S	T	S	
S	N	A	I	L		A	L	B	U	M		
M	I	S	S	O	U	R	I		R	U	E	D
U	G	H		U	S	E	S		A	C	M	E
T	H	Y		D	A	S	H		H	U	E	

ACROSS
1. Letter Z
4. Stand
8. The sun
11. Food scraps
13. Wanes
14. Top card
15. Double curve
16. Sweet courses
18. The base of a number system
20. Farewell
21. Small sandpiper
23. Optic organ
24. Prefix, over
25. Ova
27. Flaky mineral
31. Snug
33. Breakfast cereal
34. Once again
35. Leg joint
36. Type of jazz
38. Beer
39. - kwon do (Korean martial art)
41. Animals
43. Garden pest
46. Photograph book
47. State of USA
49. Regretted
52. Expression of disgust
53. Employs
54. Pinnacle
55. Your
56. Sprint
57. Colour

DOWN
1. Menagerie
2. Work unit
3. Perpetuate
4. Double-breasted overcoat
5. Mountain goat
6. Ethnic telecaster
7. Short story
8. Hindu garment
9. Prefix, eight
10. Minus
12. Marine mammal
17. Dropsy
19. Expire
21. Ship's floor
22. On top of
23. Set up
26. Needlefish
28. In view of the fact
29. Gael
30. Inspires dread
32. Abominable snowmen
37. Debutante
40. Audibly
42. Subtle emanation
43. Filth
44. Near
45. Wan
46. Greek god of war
48. America (Abbr)
50. Australian bird
51. Scottish river

solution 9

E	R	R		H	E	L	M		T	R	I
A	Y	A	H		O	G	E	E		H	A	N
R	A	N	I		L	A	I	D	B	A	C	K
		S	C	A	L	D		A	R	I	E	S
W	E	A	K	L	Y		E	L	I			
A	R	C		E	W	E	S		E	B	B	S
L	I	K	E		O	A	T		F	R	E	T
T	E	S	T		O	T	I	C		O	N	O
		H	A	D		M	A	S	A	D	A	
P	O	L	I	S		L	A	D	E	D		
S	M	A	C	K	D	A	B		A	W	A	Y
S	A	C		E	A	R	L		L	A	V	A
T	R	Y		D	Y	K	E		Y	E	P	

ACROSS
1. Go wrong
4. Tiller
8. Prefix, three
11. Indian nursemaid
13. Double curve
14. A dynasty in China
15. Indian queen
16. Nonchalant (4-4)
18. Burn with water
20. Zodiac sign
21. Feebly
23. Biblical high priest
24. Part of a circle
25. Female sheep
27. Wanes
31. Prefer
33. Breakfast cereal
34. Worry
35. Trial
36. Auricular
38. Yoko -
39. Possessed
41. Ancient fortress in Israel
43. Suffix, city
46. Loaded cargo
47. Squarely
49. Absent
52. Cyst envelope
53. Nobleman
54. Molten rock
55. Attempt
56. Levee
57. Yes

DOWN
1. Otic organ
2. Handwoven Scandinavian rug
3. Pillages
4. Tinseltown
5. Minor oath
6. Garland
7. Award of honour
8. Siamese
9. Sprint contest
10. Writing fluids
12. Rube
17. Short
19. Beer
21. - Disney
22. A Great Lake
23. Able to be estimated
26. Consume
28. Major avenue in New York City
29. Curve
30. Portico
32. Moral code
37. Bounder
40. Inquired
42. Marine mammal
43. Surreptitious, attention getting sound
44. - Khayyam
45. Lacelike
46. Songbird
48. Time of sunshine
50. Greeting
51. Yelp

solution 10

A	R	T		S	P	A	T		G	A	L
I	I	W	I		E	L	L	E		A	C	E
M	O	I	L		L	E	T	D	O	W	N	S
		T	I	N	E	A		D	U	P	E	S
O	R	C	E	I	N		F	Y	N			
R	A	H		B	I	K	E		C	H	A	P
A	N	E	W		T	O	R		E	U	R	O
D	I	S	H		E	A	T	S		M	E	R
			O	B	S		I	O	N	I	A	N
S	N	A	R	L		G	L	U	E	D		
C	A	G	L	I	A	R	I		N	I	C	K
U	N	I		S	U	E	Z		E	T	U	I
D	A	N		S	K	Y	E		Y	E	N	

ACROSS
1. Talent
4. Gaiter
8. Girl (Slang)
11. Hawaiian honeycreeper
13. Australian super-model
14. Top card
15. Drudge
16. Disappointments (3-5)
18. Athlete's foot
20. Fools
21. Red dye
23. Island of Denmark
24. Cheer
25. Bicycle
27. A bloke
31. Once again
33. Rocky peak
34. Wallaroo
35. Serving plate
36. Food
38. Sea (French)
39. Observation
41. Inhabitant of Ionia
43. Growl
46. Pasted
47. Seaport in S Sardinia
49. Notch
52. Prefix, one
53. Seaport in NE Egypt
54. Sewing case
55. Level of karate proficiency
56. Inner Hebrides island
57. Japanese currency

DOWN
1. Intention
2. - de Janeiro
3. Quick, jerky movements
4. Mythical moon-dwellers
5. Prayer
6. High-pitched
7. Woman's one-piece undergarment
8. Gape
9. Adolescent pimples
10. Minus
12. Tennis star, - Natase
17. Weight measure
19. Pen point
21. Toward the mouth
22. Indian queen
23. Enrich
26. Hawaiian acacia
28. Dampness
29. Region
30. Pornography (Colloq)
32. Verticil
37. Former coin of France
40. Ecstasy
42. Hawaiian goose
43. Driving shower
44. Grandmother
45. Against
46. Hoar
48. Diving bird
50. Prompt
51. Relation

solution 11

A	F	T		F	R	E	T		W	E	D
N	O	A	H		A	O	N	E		E	R	A
D	E	C	A		C	O	S	M	E	T	I	C
		I	V	I	E	D		P	L	A	N	E
D	E	T	E	C	T		A	T	E			
A	M	U		E	I	R	E		G	N	A	R
L	I	R	A		O	A	R		Y	A	L	E
E	R	N	E		U	P	O	N		N	O	N
			G	A	S		L	E	A	N	E	D
P	O	L	I	S		G	I	D	D	Y		
S	M	A	S	H	H	I	T		A	G	E	D
S	A	C		E	A	S	E		M	A	L	E
T	R	Y		S	O	T	S		I	L	E	

ACROSS
1. Nautical, rear
4. Worry
8. Marry
11. Ark builder
13. First class (1-3)
14. An age
15. Prefix, ten
16. Skin preparation
18. Covered with ivy
20. Wood smoothing tool
21. Notice
23. Dined
24. Atomic mass unit
25. Ireland
27. Growl
31. Italian currency
33. Paddle
34. American university
35. Sea eagle
36. On top of
38. Prefix, not
39. Vapour
41. Tilted
43. Suffix, city
46. Dizzy
47. Extremely successful play or record (5-3)
49. Old
52. Cyst envelope
53. Relax
54. Man
55. Attempt
56. Drunkards
57. Island (France)

DOWN
1. Also
2. Enemy
3. Not inclined to conversation
4. Humorous
5. Crucifix
6. Abstract being
7. Seduce
8. Scorpion-like N.Z. insect
9. Ireland
10. Fresh-water fish
12. Possess
17. Funeral oration
19. Freeze
21. Valley
22. Islamic chieftain
23. Meteors
26. Knock with knuckles
28. Redfish
29. Agave
30. Tear
32. Sponsorship
37. - Kelly
40. Australia vs England cricket trophy
42. First man
43. Surreptitious, attention getting sound
44. - Khayyam
45. Lacelike
46. Pith
48. Monetary unit of Vietnam
50. Former measure of length
51. Scottish river

solution 12

U	N	I		A	P	S	E		D	I	G
E	A	S	E		N	E	O	N		I	D	O
Y	E	L	L		A	S	S	E	S	S	O	R
		A	L	A	M	O		M	A	C	L	E
D	A	M	S	O	N		S	A	D			
U	Z	I		K	E	C	K		H	O	O	P
D	O	Z	E		S	U	E		U	R	D	U
E	V	E	N		I	D	L	E		R	E	P
			D	O	S		E	A	T	E	R	S
R	E	N	E	W		A	T	T	A	R		
A	B	E	D	N	E	G	O		R	I	P	E
R	O	T		E	R	I	N		T	E	E	S
E	N	S		D	A	N	S		S	A	P	

ACROSS
1. Prefix, one
4. Church recess
8. Excavate
11. Relax
13. Lighting gas
14. Revised form of Esperanto
15. Shout
16. Valuer
18. A poplar
20. Twinned crystal
21. Small dark-purple plum
23. Morose
24. Israeli submachine gun
25. Show disgust or strong dislike
27. Metal band
31. Nap
33. Take to court
34. Official language of Pakistan
35. Level
36. Lazy
38. Corded fabric
39. - and don'ts
41. Diners
43. Modernise
46. Fragrant oil
47. Companion of Daniel
49. Mature
52. Decay
53. Ireland
54. Golf mounds
55. Abstract being
56. Levels of karate proficiency
57. Vital tree fluid

DOWN
1. U-turn (Colloq)
2. Not
3. Convert to Islam
4. Reminiscence
5. Mexican currency
6. Distress signal
7. Purgative injection
8. Circular plate
9. Object of worship
10. Pierce with horn
12. Old cloth measures
17. Hindu ascetic
19. Very good (1-2)
21. City-dweller holidaying on a ranch
22. Northern arm of the Black Sea
23. Bones
26. Rumen
28. Planetariums
29. River in central Europe
30. Young dogs
32. Finished
37. Consume
40. Possessed
42. Pastry item
43. Uncommon
44. Black
45. Devices for fishing
46. Against
48. An age
50. Legume
51. Extrasensory perception

solution 13

T	A	J		A	D	E	N		S	H	E
O	T	I	C		C	E	R	E		M	A	Y
D	E	M	O		C	A	R	A	C	O	L	E
		D	U	P	E	D		R	I	G	O	R
S	T	A	P	E	S		L	S	D			
A	W	N		A	S	E	A		E	R	N	E
R	E	D	O		I	L	K		R	E	E	D
K	E	Y	S		O	Y	E	Z		G	A	G
			I	N	N		P	E	D	A	T	E
V	I	D	E	O		I	O	D	O	L		
A	C	E	R	B	A	T	E		E	I	R	E
N	E	B		E	D	I	T		S	T	E	M
E	S	T		L	O	S	S		Y	E	S	

ACROSS
1. - Mahal
4. Capital of Yemen
8. That woman
11. Auricular
13. Wax
14. A month
15. Demonstration
16. Wheel
18. Fooled
20. Strictness
21. Stirrup
23. Hallucinogenic drug
24. Grain beard
25. At sea
27. Sea eagle
31. Repeat
33. Family
34. Marsh plant
35. Unlocking implements
36. Town crier's call
38. To silence
39. Tavern
41. Resembling a foot
43. Television
46. Iodine solution
47. Make sour
49. Ireland
52. Beak
53. Redact
54. Stalk
55. Superlative suffix
56. Profit failure
57. Affirmative response

DOWN
1. Fox
2. Dined
3. Superior quality
4. Something added
5. Deceased
6. Go wrong
7. Draws close to
8. Polluted atmosphere
9. Nimbus
10. Looker
12. Masterstroke
17. Apple drink
19. Legume
21. Shirt
22. Affectedly dainty
23. Wordsworth, Coleridge, and Southey (4.5)
26. Cathedral city
28. Sovereignty
29. Tidy
30. Brink
32. Willow
37. Last letter
40. Prize named after inventor of dynamite
42. Performs
43. Weathercock
44. Frozen confections
45. Something owing
46. Inflammation (Suffix)
48. Fuss
50. Female ruff
51. Printer's measures

solution 14

J	O	Y		S	M	U	G		C	E	P
E	D	A	M		A	A	R	E		A	G	O
W	A	N	E		L	U	N	A	R	I	A	N
		K	A	D	A	I		R	E	N	D	S
O	P	E	N	E	D		U	S	E			
R	E	E		E	D	E	N		D	H	A	L
T	A	F	T		A	Y	E		S	O	L	E
S	K	Y	E		Y	E	A	H		L	O	N
	P	U	S		R	I	D	D	E	D		
A	L	I	E	N		S	T	E	A	D		
H	E	R	E	W	I	T	H		R	O	T	E
O	V	A		E	L	U	L		T	W	A	S
Y	I	N		D	E	N	Y		N	U	T	

ACROSS
1. Great gladness
4. Complacent
8. Brown-capped boletus mushroom
11. Dutch cheese
13. River in central Switzerland
14. In the past
15. Diminish
16. Selenographer
18. Language spoken in S China
20. Tears
21. Unlocked
23. Avail of
24. Female ruff
25. Paradise
27. Indian pulses
31. 27th president of the U.S
33. Affirmative vote
34. Foot part
35. Inner Hebrides island
36. Yes
38. Actor, - Chaney
39. Purulence
41. Disencumbered
43. Foreign
46. Place
47. Along with this
49. Routine
52. Eggs
53. 12th month of the Jewish calendar
54. It was
55. - and Yang
56. Refuse
57. Hard-shelled fruit

DOWN
1. Semite
2. Room within a harem
3. Cause to acquire Yankee traits
4. Period of youthful inexperience
5. Island in central Hawaii
6. Vase
7. Cogs
8. First son of Adam and Eve
9. Minor oath
10. Part of the brainstem
12. Intend
17. Marsh plants
19. Scottish river
21. Food scraps
22. Alp
23. Ghostly
26. Optic organ
28. Limitation
29. Agave
30. Advance money
32. Wigwam
37. Hasten
40. Unmarried
42. Blow-pipe missile
43. Nautical call
44. Son of Jacob and Leah
45. Republic in SW Asia
46. Daze
48. Island (France)
50. Greek letter
51. Superlative suffix

solution 15

P	H	I		S	C	O	W		M	A	E
A	E	R	Y		E	R	I	E		A	I	L
L	Y	R	E		D	O	L	D	R	U	M	S
		I	L	E	A	C		G	U	I	S	E
N	U	T	L	E	T		Y	E	N			
U	S	A		L	I	R	A		I	S	I	S
M	E	T	E		V	A	T		C	U	S	P
B	R	E	W		E	Y	A	S		I	L	E
		E	M	S		G	U	S	T	E	D	
A	G	G	R	O		T	H	E	T	A		
D	I	A	S	P	O	R	A		A	B	L	E
I	L	L		E	L	A	N		B	L	O	B
T	A	E		R	E	D	S		Y	O	B	

ACROSS
1. Greek letter
4. Barge
8. Actress, - West
11. Ethereal
13. A Great Lake
14. Sicken
15. Harp-like instrument
16. Region of calm winds
18. Pertaining to the ileum
20. Semblance
21. Small nut
23. Japanese currency
24. America (Abbr)
25. Italian currency
27. Egyptian goddess of fertility
31. Measure out
33. Large tub
34. Pointed end
35. Make beer
36. Nestling
38. Island (France)
39. Printer's measures
41. Blew intermittently
43. Aggression (Colloq)
46. Greek letter
47. A great dispersion of a common people
49. Capable
52. Sick
53. Dash
54. Jelly-like mass
55. - kwon do (Korean martial art)
56. Clarets
57. Teenage lout

DOWN
1. Mate
2. Attention-getting call
3. Pique
4. Tranquillisers
5. Crocodile (Colloq)
6. Lubricant
7. Chock
8. Island in central Hawaii
9. Intentions
10. Otherwise
12. Shout
17. Mysterious
19. Conger
21. Unfeeling
22. Consumer
23. Turkish swords
26. Sunbeam
28. Featly
29. Small island
30. Raced
32. Pitchers
37. Take to court
40. Sulky person
42. Pierce with knife
43. Entrance
44. Venomous lizard
45. Strong wind
46. Type of jazz
48. Bullfight call
50. Card game
51. Wane

solution 16

H	U	H			O	W	E	D		O	R	B
E	N	O	W		V	A	R	Y		W	O	O
R	I	C	E		E	D	G	I	N	E	S	S
		K	A	U	R	I		N	O	D	E	S
A	I	S	L	E	S		K	G	B			
S	O	H		Y	I	K	E		E	L	U	L
A	T	O	M		G	E	N		L	I	N	O
P	A	P	A		H	A	T	E		M	I	G
		Y	E	T		L	E	V	I	T	Y	
A	X	I	A	L		R	E	L	I	T		
C	E	N	S	O	R	E	D		V	A	A	L
E	N	S		P	A	N	G		A	R	G	O
S	O	T		E	T	T	E		Y	E	N	

ACROSS
1. Questioning exclamation
4. Was indebted
8. Sphere
11. Enough
13. Alter
14. Court
15. Staple Oriental grain
16. Nervousness
18. New Zealand evergreen tree
20. Knobs
21. Church walkways
23. Russian secret police
24. Scale note
25. Argument
27. 12th month of the Jewish calendar
31. Small particle
33. Information
34. Floor covering
35. Father
36. Detest
38. Russian plane
39. To date
41. Merriment
43. Situated on an axis
46. Rekindled
47. Having parts deleted for moral purposes
49. South African river
52. Abstract being
53. Sharp pain
54. Jason's ship
55. Drunkard
56. Suffix, diminutive
57. Japanese currency

DOWN
1. That woman
2. Prefix, one
3. Pawnshop
4. Careless omission
5. Dry riverbed
6. Work unit
7. Expiring
8. Was indebted
9. Fragrant flower
10. Employer
12. Welt
17. Prize named after inventor of dynamite
19. U-turn (Colloq)
21. As soon as possible
22. Jot
23. Scrap metal used as ballast
26. New Zealand parrot
28. Serving as a limit
29. Military detachment
30. Lethargic
32. Yucatan indians
37. Conger
40. Run off
42. Exclamation of acclaim
43. Beats by tennis service
44. Prefix, foreign
45. Current month
46. Hire
48. Rodent
50. Mature
51. Actor, - Chaney

solution 17

H	E	L		D	H	O	W		A	S	K
O	R	Y	X		R	A	P	E		N	A	N
W	A	M	E		A	N	S	E	R	I	N	E
		P	R	I	G	S		D	U	L	S	E
S	C	H	O	O	L		A	S	P			
H	A	O		N	I	C	E		E	P	E	E
I	T	I	S		N	O	R		E	R	I	N
M	O	D	E		E	D	I	T		O	R	D
		A	S	S		A	I	S	L	E	S	
S	H	A	L	E		A	L	A	M	O		
M	I	S	S	O	U	R	I		O	G	P	U
I	R	E		U	S	E	S		G	U	A	N
T	E	A		L	A	S	T		E	L	I	

ACROSS
1. Norse goddess
4. Arab vessel
8. Question
11. Large African antelope
13. Take by force
14. Grandmother
15. Belly
16. Resembling a goose
18. Prudes
20. Edible red seaweed
21. Education facility
23. Egyptian serpent
24. Monetary unit of Vietnam
25. Pleasing
27. Fencing sword
31. Inflammation (Suffix)
33. And not
34. Ireland
35. Style
36. Redact
38. W.A. river
39. Donkey
41. Church walkways
43. Fissile rock
46. A poplar
47. State of USA
49. Russian secret police
52. Anger
53. Employs
54. South American bird
55. An infusion
56. Final
57. Biblical high priest

DOWN
1. In what way?
2. An age
3. Resembling lymph
4. Large mining excavators
5. - Christian Andersen
6. Operations (colloq)
7. Unwanted plants
8. Indigo
9. Without
10. Leg joint
12. Prefix, dry
17. Indian currency
19. Charged particle
21. Spacing wedge
22. Roman censor
23. Trapeze artist
26. Food fish
28. Preface
29. Ireland
30. Finishes
32. Marine mammals
37. - Maria, coffee liqueur
40. South Korea's capital
42. Polluted atmosphere
43. Struck
44. Rent
45. At sea
46. Greek god of war
48. America (Abbr)
50. Mate
51. Prefix, one

solution 18

R	O	E			B	L	O	C		A	C	E
U	L	N	A		L	A	N	E		C	A	W
M	E	S	H		O	V	E	R	T	I	M	E
		C	O	C	O	A		E	I	D	E	R
C	L	O	Y	E	D		I	S	M			
Y	E	N		P	L	O	D		E	B	B	S
M	A	C	E		E	V	E		S	A	L	E
E	D	E	N		S	A	N	D		C	U	E
		O	P	S		T	U	S	K	E	R	
A	B	A	C	A		M	I	X	E	D		
R	A	C	H	I	T	I	C		C	O	Z	Y
A	R	E		S	U	R	A		T	O	E	A
B	E	D		A	X	E	L		R	E	P	

ACROSS
1. Fish eggs
4. Political combine
8. Top card
11. Arm bone
13. Narrow country road
14. Crow call
15. Network
16. Payment for after hours work
18. Chocolate powder
20. Downy duck
21. Satiated
23. Doctrine
24. Japanese currency
25. Walk wearily
27. Wanes
31. Club-like weapon
33. First woman
34. Bargain event
35. Paradise
36. Beach feature
38. Prompt
39. Operations (colloq)
41. Animal with tusks
43. Manila hemp plant
46. Formed by mixing
47. Having rickets
49. Snug
52. Land measure
53. Chapter of the Koran
54. New Guinea currency unit
55. Cot
56. Jump in figure skating
57. Corded fabric

DOWN
1. Odd
2. Bullfight call
3. Hide securely
4. Without blood
5. Molten rock
6. Monad
7. Roman goddess of agriculture
8. Etching fluid
9. Arrived
10. Pitcher
12. Nautical call
17. Occasions
19. Brown-capped boletus mushroom
21. Type of inflorescence
22. Heavy metal
23. The same
26. Eggs
28. Illicit method
29. Sky colour
30. Prophet
32. Methuselah's father
37. Top pupil
40. Monetary unit of India
42. Cult
43. Semite
44. Naked
45. Beaten by tennis service
46. Bog
48. Tuxedo
50. Letter Z
51. Yelp

solution 19

T	E	A		H	A	M	S		M	A	S
A	P	I	A		A	D	A	M		O	R	T
J	I	G	S		I	D	E	A	L	I	T	Y
		R	A	I	L	S		C	A	L	Y	X
A	D	E	P	T	S		S	K	I			
J	U	T		S	T	O	A		R	H	E	A
A	N	T	I		O	W	L		D	O	R	P
R	E	E	D		N	E	A	P		L	I	E
			A	T	E		C	E	A	S	E	D
A	L	P	H	A		G	I	A	N	T		
P	A	L	O	M	I	N	O		T	E	E	N
E	T	A		E	S	A	U		E	I	R	E
S	H	Y		D	A	W	S		N	A	T	

ACROSS
1. An infusion
4. Overacts
8. Mothers
11. Capital of Western Samoa
13. First man
14. Food scrap
15. Lively dances
16. Ideal quality
18. Train tracks
20. Flower part
21. Skilled people
23. Snow runner
24. Protrude
25. Portico
27. Ostrich-like bird
31. Against
33. Nocturnal bird
34. Hamlet
35. Marsh plant
36. Lowest high tide
38. Falsehood
39. Dined
41. Stopped
43. 1st letter of the Greek alphabet
46. Titan
47. Horse with a golden coat
49. Adolescent
52. Greek letter
53. Son of Isaac and Rebekah
54. Ireland
55. Timid
56. Black birds
57. Singer, - "King" Cole

DOWN
1. - Mahal
2. Prefix, over
3. Plume
4. Pellet of hail
5. Appends
6. Actress, - West
7. Hit
8. Drudge
9. Ostentatious
10. River of Hades
12. As soon as possible
17. Scottish lord
19. Sexless things
21. Slightly open
22. Sand hill
23. Lecherous
26. Be indebted
28. Breed of dairy cattle
29. A Great Lake
30. Mimicked
32. State in the NW United States
37. Legume
40. Domesticated
42. Poker stake
43. Primates
44. Slat
45. Stage show
46. Chew on a bone
48. Mount - , N.W. Qld. mining town
50. An age
51. Seine

solution 20

D	E	R		F	A	N	G		V	A	T
O	V	A	L		O	G	E	E		O	D	E
M	E	N	U		R	O	B	O	T	I	Z	E
		K	L	I	E	G		D	U	D	E	S
D	O	L	L	A	R		G	E	M			
O	B	I		M	E	S	H		I	D	O	L
O	I	N	K		A	P	E		D	A	T	A
M	E	G	A		C	A	T	O		F	I	T
		U	G	H		T	H	A	T	C	H	
I	N	F	R	A		W	O	M	E	N		
B	E	R	I	B	E	R	I		R	E	A	D
I	S	A		O	Y	E	Z		O	S	L	O
S	T	Y		N	E	N	E		S	B	S	

ACROSS
1. The (German)
4. Viper's tooth
8. Large tub
11. Egg-shaped
13. Double curve
14. Poem
15. List of dishes
16. Turn into a robot
18. Bright arc light
20. Dandies
21. Monetary unit
23. Jewel
24. Japanese sash
25. Network
27. Object of worship
31. Hog sound
33. Primate
34. Information
35. Prefix, large
36. Roman censor
38. Spasm
39. Expression of disgust
41. Roof with straw
43. Below
46. Adult females
47. Vitamin deficiency disease
49. Peruse
52. Mount - , N.W. Qld. mining town
53. Town crier's call
54. Capital of Norway
55. Pig enclosure
56. Hawaiian goose
57. Ethnic telecaster

DOWN
1. Benedictine monk's title
2. First woman
3. Festering
4. Maintain headway
5. Eager
6. Beak
7. Rock cavity
8. Empty
9. Hoe-shaped axe
10. Golf mounds
12. Soothe
17. Swollen
19. Braggart (Colloq) (1.2)
21. Fate
22. Off-Broadway theater award
23. Segregate in a ghetto
26. Mineral spring
28. Foolishness
29. Auricular
30. Slat
32. New Zealand evergreen tree
37. Electrical resistance unit
40. Republic in W equatorial Africa
42. Prefix, air
43. Sacred Egyptian bird
44. Nidus
45. Ravel
46. Songbird
48. Optic organ
50. Long-sleeved linen vestment
51. - and don'ts

solution 21

F	O	X		E	C	H	O		E	B	B
I	R	A	N		R	I	O	T		Y	E	A
N	E	N	E		R	A	P	T	U	R	E	D
		T	A	B	O	O		E	L	A	T	E
T	E	H	R	A	N		A	R	C			
O	D	A		H	E	M	S		E	R	N	S
T	A	T	A		O	R	C		R	E	A	P
O	M	E	N		U	S	E	D		A	M	U
			G	A	S		N	U	R	S	E	R
R	E	A	L	M		I	D	E	A	S		
E	U	P	E	P	S	I	A		G	I	B	E
A	R	E		L	A	W	N		A	G	E	S
M	O	D		E	D	I	T		N	E	T	

ACROSS
1. Sly animal
4. Reverberate
8. Wane
11. Republic in SW Asia
13. Uproar
14. Yes
15. Hawaiian goose
16. Mentally transported
18. Forbidden
20. Overjoy
21. Capital of Iran
23. Part of a circle
24. Room within a harem
25. Garment edges
27. Sea eagles
31. Good-bye (2-2)
33. Killer whale
34. Harvest
35. Portent
36. Second-hand
38. Atomic mass unit
39. Vapour
41. Suckler
43. Kingdom
46. Notions
47. Good digestion
49. Deride
52. Land measure
53. Grass around house
54. Matures
55. Very modern
56. Redact
57. Seine

DOWN
1. Fish part
2. Crude mineral
3. Salt of xanthic acid
4. Mistaken
5. Goodbye
6. Jump
7. Marine mammal
8. Jaguarundi
9. Root vegetable
10. Past tense of bid
12. Close to
17. Peptic complaint
19. Expression of contempt
21. In -, in all
22. Dutch cheese
23. An ancestor
26. Missus
28. Reallocate
29. Title
30. Goad
32. Fish
37. Owing
40. Sufficient
42. Hindu music
43. Quantity of paper
44. Wallaroo
45. Mimicked
46. Hawaiian honeycreeper
48. Morose
50. Hive insect
51. Superlative suffix

solution 22

N	A	G			D	E	L	L		O	D	E
I	D	E	M		E	L	S	E		C	O	Y	
N	O	N	O		C	A	D	A	S	T	E	R
		O	R	I	O	N		S	P	O	R	E
V	E	C	T	O	R			L	E	A		
A	N	I		N	A	R	Y		C	A	T	O
L	O	D	E		T	I	A		E	B	O	N
E	W	E	S		E	M	M	Y		R	U	T
		S	O	D		H	E	P	A	T	O	
G	A	N	E	F		M	O	A	T	S		
H	A	U	S	F	R	A	U		A	I	D	E
A	R	K		A	Y	I	N		H	O	E	S
T	E	E		L	A	N	D		N	E	T	

ACROSS
1. Henpeck
4. Small valley
8. Poem
11. As previously given
13. Otherwise
14. Bashful
15. Something not to be done (2-2)
16. Real estate register
18. The Hunter
20. Fern seed
21. Disease carrier
23. Meadow
24. Black bird
25. Never
27. Roman censor
31. Ore deposit
33. - Maria, coffee liqueur
34. Black
35. Female sheep
36. U.S. TV award
38. Groove
39. Soil
41. Prefix, liver
43. Swindler
46. Water filled defences
47. Housewife
49. Assistant
52. Noah's vessel
53. 16th letter of the Hebrew alphabet
54. Gardening tools
55. Golf peg
56. Come to ground
57. Seine

DOWN
1. A fool
2. Fuss
3. Racial extermination
4. Adorned
5. Dash
6. Hallucinogenic drug
7. Rent agreement
8. Prefix, eight
9. Performer
10. Australian explorer
12. Three-year-old salmon
17. Room
19. Charged particle
21. Valley
22. Enough
23. Bloodhound
26. Edge
28. Scraped spot or area
29. Solicit
30. Upon
32. S-bends
37. Yes
40. Liver, kidneys or tripe
42. Egyptian deity
43. Steps descending to a river
44. River in central Switzerland
45. Use atomic bom on (Colloq)
46. Chief
48. Handwoven Scandinavian rug
50. Scottish river
51. Superlative suffix

solution 23

U	S	A		S	I	K	H		A	U	K
H	O	L	M		I	D	E	A		P	S	I
F	U	M	E		N	E	A	R	M	I	S	S
		I	N	D	U	S		R	E	A	R	S
R	O	G	U	E	S		G	Y	M			
U	G	H		E	I	R	E		O	U	C	H
S	E	T	A		T	O	N		S	L	U	E
K	E	Y	S		I	C	E	D		T	R	I
		T	I	S		R	A	P	I	E	R	
S	A	L	E	M		S	A	L	E	M		
H	A	I	R	B	A	L	L		G	A	G	A
U	R	N		U	R	A	L		S	T	I	R
T	E	N		E	M	M	Y		E	T	C	

ACROSS
1. America (Abbr)
4. Hindu sect
8. Diving bird
11. Ilex
13. Notion
14. Pressure symbol
15. Vapour
16. Not a direct hit
18. Indian river
20. Brings up
21. Bounders
23. Gymnasium
24. Expression of disgust
25. Ireland
27. Ornamental brooch
31. Bristle
33. Heavy weight
34. Swing around
35. Unlocking implements
36. Decorated cake
38. Prefix, three
39. It is
41. Fencing sword
43. American witch hunt city
46. American witch hunt city
47. Ball of hair
49. Insane
52. Vase
53. European mountain range
54. Agitate
55. Decade
56. U.S. TV award
57. Etcetera

DOWN
1. Television frequency
2. Former coin of France
3. God
4. Sinus inflammation
5. Roman dates
6. New Zealand parrot
7. Annoy
8. Capital of Western Samoa
9. Former Soviet Union
10. Osculate
12. List of dishes
17. Brief notes
19. Scottish river
21. Teething biscuit
22. Double curve
23. Ordinarily
26. Fabulous bird
28. Eventual
29. Remedy
30. Scion
32. Flower
37. Indian dish
40. Dye
42. Clothesline clips
43. Closed
44. River in central Switzerland
45. Waterfall
46. Close hard
48. Limb
50. British, a fool
51. Part of a circle

solution 24

C	U	P	■	D	H	A	L	■	T	E	T
U	S	E	D	■	A	O	N	E	■	E	R	A
B	E	A	R	■	V	O	T	A	R	E	S	S
■	■	C	I	V	E	T	■	V	A	N	E	S
D	E	E	P	E	N	■	L	E	I	■	■	■
O	A	F	■	E	P	E	E	■	L	A	G	S
D	R	U	B	■	O	V	A	■	S	C	A	T
O	L	L	A	■	R	E	D	D	■	C	O	Y
■	■	■	N	U	T	■	L	A	B	I	L	E
S	E	E	K	S	■	O	I	L	E	D	■	■
P	U	R	S	U	I	N	G	■	E	E	L	S
E	R	G	■	A	R	C	H	■	S	N	A	P
D	O	S	■	L	E	E	T	■	T	E	A	■

ACROSS
1. Drinking vessel
4. Indian pulses
8. 9th letter of the Hebrew alphabet
11. Second-hand
13. First class (1-3)
14. An age
15. Ursa
16. Woman who is a votary
18. Musk-yielding cat
20. Weathercocks
21. Become more intense
23. Garland
24. Clumsy person
25. Fencing sword
27. Delays
31. Thrash
33. Eggs
34. Shoo
35. Earthen pot
36. Spawning area of salmon
38. Bashful
39. Hard-shelled fruit
41. Likely to change
43. Searches for
46. Lubricated
47. Pursuant
49. Long fish
52. Work unit
53. Curved entrance
54. Break suddenly
55. - and don'ts
56. English court
57. An infusion

DOWN
1. Young bear
2. Avail of
3. Free from strife
4. Type of sofa
5. Loud derisory cry
6. Social insect
7. Depart
8. Adolescent
9. Gaelic
10. Soviet news service
12. Drop moisture
17. Train tracks
19. Victory sign
21. Extinct bird
22. Nobleman
23. Decorative window pane
26. First woman
28. Chance
29. Jail
30. Eye inflammation
32. Financial institutions
37. Indian dish
40. Customary
42. Hive insects
43. Raced
44. Wallaroo
45. Work units
46. At one time
48. Anger
50. New Guinea seaport
51. Mineral spring

solution 25

G	A	Y		H	I	C	K		H	E	L
A	L	A	R		A	S	E	A		O	V	A
L	E	T	O		I	N	T	R	E	P	I	D
		A	T	I	L	T		A	N	I	L	E
O	R	G	A	N	S		E	T	A			
A	A	H		S	T	A	B		C	H	O	P
K	N	A	P		O	H	O		T	U	T	U
S	I	N	O		N	A	N	A		G	I	N
			U	S	E		I	N	D	U	C	T
S	P	A	R	K		A	S	I	D	E		
H	E	L	S	I	N	K	I		A	N	T	I
I	R	E		R	E	I	N		Y	O	W	L
V	E	E		L	O	N	G		T	A	E	

ACROSS
1. Merry
4. Rube
8. Norse goddess
11. Having wings
13. At sea
14. Eggs
15. Mother of Apollo
16. Brave
18. Leaning
20. Old womanish
21. Keyboard instruments
23. Greek letter
24. Exclamation of surprise
25. Pierce with knife
27. Hew
31. Summit of a small hill
33. Exclamation of surprise
34. Ballet skirt
35. Prefix, Chinese
36. Grandmother
38. Rummy game
39. Avail of
41. Introduce
43. Electric discharge
46. Stage whisper
47. Capital of Finland
49. Against
52. Anger
53. Riding strap
54. Howl
55. Victory sign
56. Lengthy
57. - kwon do (Korean martial art)

DOWN
1. Girl (Slang)
2. Beer
3. Turkish sword
4. Pellet of hail
5. Is not
6. Prefix, whale
7. Unit for measuring gold
8. American Indian
9. Sinister
10. Burden
12. Roster
17. Make law
19. - and outs, intricacies
21. Large trees
22. Indian queen
23. Finishing in imitation of ebony
26. Exclamation of surprise
28. French Protestant
29. Auricular
30. Bet
32. Decants
37. Black bird
40. Bagpipe sound
42. June 6, 1944
43. Switchblade
44. Father
45. To the sheltered side
46. Related
48. Prefix, new
50. Two
51. Island (France)

solution 26

B	A	L	M		A	F	R	O		A	R	T
E	P	E	E		L	A	O	S		C	H	E
N	E	T	S		P	R	E	P		M	E	N
			H	O	H	O		R	H	E	A	S
M	A	C	U	L	A		T	E	E			
A	D	A	G	E		C	R	Y		E	O	S
C	A	N	A		K	O	I		U	R	T	I
E	R	E		D	E	R		S	T	A	I	N
	O	A	F		K	I	T	S	C	H		
L	E	A	R	N		S	A	N	E			
A	W	L		G	U	L	F		R	A	S	P
C	E	P		E	S	A	U		E	G	O	S
E	R	S		R	A	G	E		D	E	L	I

ACROSS
1. Ointment
5. Frizzy hair style
9. Talent
12. Fencing sword
13. South-east Asian nation
14. - Guevara
15. Devices for fishing
16. Prepare patient for operation
17. Soldiers
18. Laughing sound (2.2)
20. Ostrich-like birds
22. Spot on the skin
25. Golf peg
26. Maxim
27. Bawl
28. Greek goddess of the dawn
31. Scene of first miracle
32. Colorful form of the common carp
33. Upper respiratory tract infection
34. Before
35. The (German)
36. Blemish
37. Clumsy person
38. Something of tawdry design
39. Find out
42. Sensible
43. Shoemaker's tool
44. Large bay
46. Grate
50. Brown-capped boletus mushroom
51. Son of Isaac and Rebekah
52. Personalities
53. Bitter vetch
54. Storm
55. Delicatessen

DOWN
1. Scottish hill
2. Primate
3. Allow
4. Crazy
5. 1st letter of the Greek alphabet
6. Gambling game
7. Fish eggs
8. Fish-hawk
9. Pinnacle
10. Ostrich-like bird
11. Decades
19. Bullfight call
21. Masculine pronoun
22. Club-like weapon
23. 6th month of the Jewish calendar
24. Rattan
25. Prefix, three
27. Minced oath
28. Periods of history
29. Auricular
30. Hyperbolic sine
32. State of drowsy contentment
33. Spoke
35. Peril
36. Transgress
37. Otherwise
38. River in Zambia
39. Openwork fabric
40. Pitcher
41. Peaks
42. Metal dross
45. America (Abbr)
47. Mature
48. The sun
49. Pressure symbol

solution 27

D	O	P	E	■	S	K	A	W	■	H	E	M
A	B	E	D	■	L	E	T	O	■	O	L	E
B	I	N	D	■	O	N	E	R	■	H	U	T
■	■	■	Y	O	K	O	■	D	H	O	L	E
N	O	T	I	C	E	■	S	E	E	■	■	■
A	R	E	N	A	■	K	I	D	■	L	E	K
S	T	A	G	■	C	O	P	■	L	O	P	E
A	S	K	■	M	I	A	■	P	O	S	E	R
■	■	■	H	O	D	■	L	O	O	T	E	R
F	L	A	I	L	■	B	I	T	S	■	■	■
O	U	D	■	D	A	R	T	■	E	L	A	N
N	A	E	■	E	V	E	R	■	L	O	B	E
T	U	N	■	R	E	D	E	■	Y	O	Y	O

ACROSS
1. Drugs
5. Skagen
9. Garment edge
12. In bed
13. Mother of Apollo
14. Bullfight call
15. Tie
16. Unique thing
17. Cabin
18. - Ono
20. Wild Asian dog
22. See
25. Witness
26. Stadium
27. Young goat
28. Monetary unit of Albania
31. Male deer
32. Policeman
33. Bound
34. Question
35. Actress, - Farrow
36. Difficult question
37. Brick carrier
38. Plunderer
39. Thresh
42. Fragments
43. Musical instrument
44. Blow-pipe missile
46. Dash
50. Not
51. Always
52. Ear part
53. Large barrel
54. Advise
55. Stringed toy

DOWN
1. Skilled
2. Japanese sash
3. Female swan
4. Swirling
5. Seaweed
6. Lotto-like gambling game
7. Dined
8. Phrased
9. Laughing sound (2.2)
10. 12th month of the Jewish calendar
11. Measure out
19. Wood sorrel
21. Masculine pronoun
22. U.S. space agency
23. Food scraps
24. Timber tree
25. Small drink
27. Hawaiian acacia
28. Was defeated
29. Fencing sword
30. Former Governor General, Sir John -
32. Spanish hero
33. Slackly
35. Crumble
36. Cooking implement
37. Hello there
38. Fluid measure
39. Baptismal vessel
40. Hawaiian feast
41. Capital of Yemen
42. Reared
45. Greeting
47. Card game
48. To endure
49. Prefix, new

solution 28

N	E	E	D		C	H	A	T		R	A	W
O	G	R	E		R	O	D	E		I	L	E
G	O	A	D		O	B	O	E		N	O	D
			U	N	C	O		H	I	D	E	S
S	A	U	C	E	S		C	E	T			
C	A	R	T	E		P	R	E		S	P	A
A	R	E	S		I	O	U		C	A	U	L
T	E	A		M	O	A		J	O	U	L	E
			S	I	N		G	A	R	L	I	C
C	O	C	O	A		D	O	G	S			
H	A	O		S	K	A	W		A	S	E	A
A	H	A		M	I	C	A		G	U	L	F
P	U	L		A	D	E	N		E	M	I	T

ACROSS
1. Require
5. Natter
9. Uncooked
12. Monster
13. Travelled on
14. Island (France)
15. Spur
16. Hautboy
17. Indicate assent
18. Remarkable
20. Finds shelter
22. Condiments
25. Prefix, whale
26. Menu
27. Prefix, before
28. Mineral spring
31. Greek god of war
32. Acknowledgement of debt
33. Hood-like membrane
34. An infusion
35. New Zealand bird
36. Unit of energy
37. Transgress
38. Pungent bulb plant
39. Chocolate powder
42. Canines
43. Monetary unit of Vietnam
44. Skagen
46. At sea
50. Exclamation of surprise
51. Flaky mineral
52. Large bay
53. Monetary unit of Afghanistan
54. Capital of Yemen
55. Send out

DOWN
1. Egg drink
2. The self
3. An age
4. Subtracts
5. Crocodiles (Colloq)
6. Tramp
7. Fuss
8. Titter
9. Skin
10. Agave
11. Marries
19. Born
21. Neuter singular pronoun
22. Shoo
23. River in central Switzerland
24. Fertiliser
25. French vineyard
27. Price on application (Abbr)
28. First king of Israel
29. Hungarian sheepdog
30. Smart - , show-off
32. Charged particle
33. Small bouquet
35. Poisonous effluvia
36. Sharp projection
37. Therefore
38. Daisy
39. A bloke
40. Island of Hawaii
41. Ember
42. Fresh-water fish
45. Young goat
47. Total
48. Biblical high priest
49. Nautical, rear

solution 29

P	U	N	S	■	S	P	I	T	■	T	H	E
I	L	I	E	■	H	A	L	E	■	O	A	R
E	T	N	A	■	A	L	E	C	■	F	R	O
■	■	■	L	A	M	P	■	T	H	U	D	S
F	O	R	A	G	E	■	C	U	E	■	■	■
L	L	A	N	O	■	T	A	M	■	T	A	U
E	D	G	E	■	N	O	B	■	F	E	S	S
A	S	S	■	N	E	D	■	T	E	N	T	S
■	■	■	D	O	E	■	S	A	N	T	I	R
H	O	B	O	S	■	C	U	E	D	■	■	■
A	G	E	■	T	R	A	M	■	E	T	C	H
I	L	L	■	R	O	M	E	■	R	A	R	E
R	E	T	■	A	C	E	R	■	S	P	U	N

ACROSS
1. Plays on words
5. Expectorate
9. Definite article
12. Tennis star, - Natase
13. Robust
14. Paddle
15. Sicilian volcano
16. Smart - , show-off
17. To and -
18. Torch
20. Dull sounds
22. Rummage
25. Prompt
26. Grassy plain
27. Scottish cap
28. Greek letter
31. Brink
32. Jack in cribbage
33. Heraldry, wide horizontal stripe on shield
34. Donkey
35. - Kelly
36. Camp shelters
37. Female deer
38. Persian musical instrument
39. Tramps
42. Prompted
43. Mature
44. Railed public transport
46. Engrave with acid
50. Sick
51. Italian capital
52. Uncommon
53. Soak flax
54. The maple
55. Reeled

DOWN
1. Pastry item
2. Last month
3. A fool
4. Shipping route (3.4)
5. Disgrace
6. Insect feeler
7. Island (France)
8. Rooflike structure
9. Beancurd
10. Difficult
11. Greek god of love
19. In the past
21. Masculine pronoun
22. Parasitic insect
23. One's parents (Colloq)
24. Torn clothing
25. Taxi
27. Fox
28. Camp shelter
29. Italian wine province
30. Former Soviet Union
32. Born
33. Automobile wheelguards
35. Cosa -, American Mafia
36. - kwon do (Korean martial art)
37. Perform
38. Ancient region in S Mesopotamia
39. Tress
40. Leer
41. Leather strap
42. Arrived
45. Fabulous bird
47. Faucet
48. French vineyard
49. Female bird

solution 30

Puzzle 1

M	E	O	W		D	H	A	L		S	P	A
E	Y	R	A		R	I	V	E		L	O	X
M	E	T	E		O	G	E	E		A	R	E
			S	I	N	H		R	A	W	E	R
V	O	L	U	T	E		S	E	N			
A	L	E	C	S		Z	E	D		B	O	W
S	I	N	K		Z	I	T		R	A	L	E
T	O	T		C	E	P		A	I	S	L	E
			M	A	E		M	I	S	H	A	P
R	A	V	E	N		M	A	R	S			
E	L	I		A	Y	A	H		O	P	U	S
C	O	N		P	E	N	D		L	I	R	E
K	E	A		E	T	U	I		E	T	N	A

ACROSS
1. Sound of a cat
5. Indian pulses
9. Mineral spring
12. Jaguarundi
13. Split
14. Brine-cured salmon
15. Measure out
16. Double curve
17. Land measure
18. Hyperbolic sine
20. Less cooked
22. Spiral formation
25. Monetary unit of Japan
26. Smart - , show-offs
27. Last letter
28. Bend
31. Subside
32. Acne pimple
33. Death rattle
34. Young child
35. Brown-capped boletus mushroom
36. Church walkway
37. Actress, - West
38. Accident
39. Black bird
42. Red planet
43. Biblical high priest
44. Indian nursemaid
46. Musical work
50. Cheat
51. Hang
52. Italian currency
53. New Zealand parrot
54. Sewing case
55. Sicilian volcano

DOWN
1. 13th letter of the Hebrew alphabet
2. Optic organ
3. Food scrap
4. Alas
5. Male bee
6. Lofty
7. Greeting
8. Ogled
9. Cabbage salad
10. Skin opening
11. Woodman
19. Sexless things
21. Prefix meaning without
22. Extensive
23. Potpourri
24. Time of abstinence
25. Become firm
27. Toothed fastener
28. Hit hard
29. Earthen pot
30. Sob
32. Letter Z
33. Meatball
35. Hors d'oeuvre
36. Atmosphere
37. Objective case of I
38. Muslim messiah
39. To matter
40. Agave
41. Musical instrument of India
42. Hindu lawgiver
45. To date
47. Mine
48. Vase
49. Large body of water

Puzzle 2

L	A	U	D		B	E	E	T		N	O	B
A	R	E	A		R	E	E	L		E	G	O
B	E	Y	S		U	L	N	A		T	E	A
			Y	A	M	S		L	A	S	E	R
D	A	N	U	B	E		B	O	N			
H	O	A	R	Y		L	A	C		S	E	T
A	N	T	E		P	E	A		R	A	R	E
L	E	O		T	E	D		A	E	R	I	E
			B	A	G		E	D	D	I	E	S
C	H	E	E	P		C	R	O	C			
O	I	L		E	C	H	O		O	A	K	S
O	V	A		R	A	I	D		A	N	E	W
P	E	N		S	Y	C	E		T	I	N	Y

ACROSS
1. Praise
5. Root vegetable
9. Jack in cribbage
12. Region
13. Spool
14. The self
15. Turkish governors
16. Arm bone
17. An infusion
18. Sweet potatoes
20. Light beam
22. Austrian river
25. French, good
26. Grey
27. Resinous deposit
28. Become firm
31. Poker stake
32. Legume
33. Uncommon
34. Zodiac sign
35. Spread out for drying
36. Eagle's nest
37. Sack
38. Whirlpools
39. Chirp
42. Crocodile (Colloq)
43. Lubricant
44. Reverberate
46. Large trees
50. Eggs
51. Incursion
52. Once again
53. Female swan
54. Stable attendant
55. Wee

DOWN
1. Laboratory
2. Land measure
3. U-turn (Colloq)
4. Carnivorous marsupial
5. Mist
6. Long fish
7. Even (poet.)
8. Aztec god of rain
9. Devices for fishing
10. Double curve
11. Hog
19. To endure
21. Prefix meaning without
22. Indian pulses
23. First class (1-3)
24. Western pact
25. Bleat
27. Captained
28. Hindu garment
29. A Great Lake
30. Golf mounds
32. Wooden pin
33. Historically, a British soldier
35. Becomes narrow
36. Fuss
37. To exist
38. Wear away
39. Fowl enclosure
40. Bee nest
41. Dash
42. Stylish
45. Coral island
47. Black bird
48. Knowledge
49. Two-up

solution 31

C	E	R	E		N	E	N	E		O	D	A
I	L	E	X		A	G	I	N		C	O	N
D	I	E	S		P	O	N	D		T	N	T
			C	U	P	S		U	S	A	G	E
R	E	V	I	L	E		G	E	O			
A	G	E	N	T		A	I	D		D	E	R
C	O	E	D		R	I	B		F	R	A	U
E	S	P		C	O	L		E	R	A	S	E
			A	R	C		T	E	A	T	E	D
S	H	A	M	E		B	A	L	I			
A	O	K		A	Y	A	H		L	O	C	H
U	N	I		K	O	L	O		E	C	H	O
L	E	N		Y	U	L	E		R	A	I	D

ACROSS
1. Wax
5. Hawaiian goose
9. Room within a harem
12. Holly
13. Against
14. Cheat
15. Ceases living
16. Pool
17. An explosive
18. Drinking vessels
20. Consumption
22. Malign
25. Prefix, the earth
26. Spy
27. Assist
28. The (German)
31. Student at mixed school
32. Chest bone
33. German Mrs
34. Extrasensory perception
35. Mountain pass
36. Rub out
37. Part of a circle
38. Having nipples
39. Disgrace
42. Indonesian resort island
43. Very good (1-2)
44. Indian nursemaid
46. Scottish lake
50. Prefix, one
51. Serbian folk dance
52. Reverberate
53. Pet form of Leonard
54. Christmas
55. Incursion

DOWN
1. Spanish hero
2. Biblical high priest
3. Female ruff
4. Cut out
5. One of the two equal sections of a cone
6. Personalities
7. A fool
8. Invested
9. Prefix, eight
10. Hit or punch (Colloq)
11. Poker stake
19. Last month
21. Therefore
22. Sprint contest
23. Personalities
24. Vice president
25. Castrated male cat
27. Sicken
28. Minor oath
29. Relax
30. Regretted
32. Fabulous bird
33. More feeble
35. Dilapidated
36. Conger
37. Part of the verb "to be"
38. Lake in the Sierra Nevada
39. First king of Israel
40. Sharpen
41. Related
42. Formal dance
45. Yourself
47. Wood sorrel
48. Greek letter
49. Brick carrier

solution 32

G	A	M	Y	■	H	Y	P	E	■	G	A	L
E	P	E	E	■	E	M	I	R	■	E	G	O
L	E	T	S	■	L	I	P	S	■	N	E	D
■			H	A	I	R		A	B	U	S	E
M	E	D	I	C	O	■	U	T	E			
O	G	I	V	E	■	F	E	Z	■	B	O	O
J	A	V	A	■	B	A	Y	■	D	O	R	M
O	D	A	■	F	I	N	■	B	R	A	Z	E
■			H	O	B	■	O	R	I	S	O	N
B	A	B	E	R	■	S	C	A	B	■		
R	U	E	■	U	T	A	H	■	B	O	O	R
I	R	E	■	M	O	R	E	■	L	U	B	E
O	A	F	■	S	T	I	R	■	E	R	S	E

ACROSS
1. Tasting like wild fowl
5. Stimulate
9. Girl (Slang)
12. Fencing sword
13. Islamic chieftain
14. The self
15. Allows
16. Edges
17. - Kelly
18. Tress
20. Ill-treat
22. Physician
25. Small truck
26. Pointed arch
27. Turkish cap
28. Jeer
31. Main island of Indonesia
32. Cove
33. College residential building
34. Room within a harem
35. Fish part
36. Solder
37. Fireplace ledge
38. Prayer
39. Founder of the Mogul Empire
42. Strike breaker
43. Regret
44. American state
46. Dull person
50. Anger
51. Extra
52. Lubricate
53. Clumsy person
54. Agitate
55. Gaelic

DOWN
1. Congeal
2. Primate
3. Greeted
4. Orthodox Jewish school
5. Prefix, sun
6. Primordial giant in Norse myth
7. Fruit seed
8. As a substitute
9. Knee
10. Matures
11. Ore deposit
19. Top card
21. To exist
22. Voodoo amulet
23. Minor oath
24. Prima donna
25. U-turn (Colloq)
27. Avid admirer
28. Large snakes
29. Ricelike grains of pasta
30. Portent
32. Infant's protective garment
33. Slobber
35. Tribunals
36. Brassiere
37. Masculine pronoun
38. Red earth pigment
39. Vigor
40. Subtle emanation
41. Cow flesh
42. Hindu garment
45. Young child
47. Of us
48. Observation
49. Female ruff

solution 33

W	A	M	E	■	B	Y	T	E	A	R	C
A	L	A	R	■	O	A	R	S	■	S	U	R
X	E	N	O	■	S	N	I	P	■	E	G	O
■			D	O	U	G	■	I	S	A	A	C
S	I	M	I	A	N	■	G	E	O	■
P	L	O	N	K	■	F	A	D	■	S	A	P
R	I	N	G	■	Q	E	D	■	H	A	L	E
Y	A	O	■	C	U	E	■	N	U	R	S	E
■			P	Y	A	■	C	A	M	I	O	N
X	E	R	I	C	■	I	R	E	D	■
E	V	E	■	L	U	T	E	■	R	O	R	T
R	I	D	■	I	T	I	S	■	U	P	O	N
O	L	D	■	C	E	S	T	■	M	E	E	T

ACROSS
1. Belly
5. Unit of computer memory
9. Part of a circle
12. Having wings
13. Paddles
14. Prefix, over
15. Prefix, foreign
16. Pare
17. The self
18. Cricketer, - Walters
20. Son of Abraham
22. Of apes
25. Prefix, the earth
26. Fall heavily
27. A craze
28. Vital tree fluid
31. Encircle
32. Which was to be proved
33. Robust
34. Legendary emperor of China
35. Prompt
36. Nurture
37. Monetary unit of Burma
38. Dray
39. Adapted to a dry environment
42. Angered
43. First woman
44. Stringed instrument
46. Cheat the system
50. Free
51. Inflammation (Suffix)
52. On top of
53. Aged
54. Girdle
55. Greet

DOWN
1. Bee product
2. Beer
3. Human race
4. Wearing
5. Boatswain
6. Yin and -
7. Prefix, three
8. Glimpsed
9. At sea
10. Wrinkle
11. Crocodile (Colloq)
19. Large tree
21. Therefore
22. Agile
23. Hip bones
24. Prefix, one
25. Goad for driving cattle
27. A charge
28. Hindu garment
29. As well as
30. Hammer head
32. As
33. Boring
35. Recurring in cycles
36. Not
37. The ratio between circumference and diameter
38. Plume
39. Prefix, dry
40. Sinister
41. Spawning area of salmon
42. Inflammation (Suffix)
45. Small truck
47. Open
48. Fish eggs
49. An explosive

solution 34

P	O	K	Y		S	N	I	P		T	O	G
A	L	O	E		O	A	T	H		A	P	E
Y	E	A	R		U	R	S	A		L	E	E
			E	S	P	Y		S	H	A	C	K
S	L	A	V	E	S		Z	E	E			
L	I	L	A	C		S	I	S		D	D	T
A	K	I	N		C	A	P		A	U	R	A
V	E	T		F	E	Y		I	L	L	E	R
		A	L	P		I	N	G	L	E	S	
S	E	A	M	Y		A	O	N	E			
I	L	L		R	A	N	D		B	O	O	M
D	A	M		O	L	I	O		R	I	V	E
E	N	S		D	E	L	L		A	L	A	R

ACROSS
1. Small and cramped
5. Pare
9. To clothe
12. Agave
13. Vow
14. Primate
15. Long period of time
16. Bear constellation
17. Sheltered side
18. Glimpse
20. Shanty
22. Bondsmen
25. Letter Z
26. Fragrant flower
27. Sister
28. Once common, now banned, insecticide
31. Related
32. Item of headwear
33. Subtle emanation
34. Examine thoroughly
35. Doomed
36. Sicker
37. Peak
38. Fireplaces
39. Sordid
42. First class (1-3)
43. Sick
44. South African currency
46. Time of prosperity
50. Weir
51. Potpourri
52. Split
53. Abstract being
54. Small valley
55. Having wings

DOWN
1. Wages
2. Bullfight call
3. Hawaiian acacia
4. Capital of Armenia
5. Broths
6. Never
7. Sexless things
8. Stages
9. Monetary unit of Western Samoa
10. Oil cartel
11. Strange person
19. Dry (wine)
21. Masculine pronoun
22. European race
23. Prefer
24. Got down from mount
25. Toothed fastener
27. Utter
28. Lustreless
29. Endure
30. Sailors
32. Brown-capped boletus mushroom
33. Branch of mathematics
35. Fishing rod
36. Tavern
37. Part of the verb "to be"
38. Iodine solution
39. Team
40. Dash
41. Charity
42. Indigo
45. Beer
47. Lubricant
48. Eggs
49. Sea (French)

solution 35

G	N	U	S	■	A	C	H	E	■	O	V	A
Y	E	R	K	■	Z	O	O	M	■	G	I	N
M	O	N	A	■	T	I	D	E	■	E	L	I
■	■	■	■	T	R	E	F	■	S	T	E	E	L
M	A	N	I	A	C	■	■	R	I	O	■	■
E	B	O	N	Y	■	■	U	P	S	■	G	I	T
S	U	N	G	■	H	E	M	■	S	I	D	E
A	T	E	■	L	E	Y	■	O	U	Z	E	L
■	■	■	S	O	W	■	M	A	D	A	M	E
E	L	B	O	W	■	S	U	R	A	■	■	■
D	I	E	■	I	M	P	S	■	N	I	K	E
A	N	T	■	N	O	A	H	■	I	L	I	A
M	E	S	■	G	O	R	Y	■	C	E	N	T

ACROSS
1. Wildebeest
5. Pain
9. Eggs
12. Arouse
13. Move rapidly
14. Rummy game
15. - Lisa
16. Ocean fluctuation
17. Biblical high priest
18. Not kosher
20. Iron product
22. Madman
25. - de Janeiro
26. Black wood
27. Raises
28. British, a fool
31. Carolled
32. Garment edge
33. Team
34. Dined
35. Arable land temporarily sown with grass
36. Thrush
37. Female pig
38. Title for a woman
39. Arm joint
42. Chapter of the Koran
43. Expire
44. Little devils
46. Goddess of victory
50. Social insect
51. Ark builder
52. Hip bones
53. My, French (Plural)
54. Bloody
55. Monetary unit

DOWN
1. Gymnasium
2. Prefix, new
3. Vase
4. Performing on ice
5. Indian of Mexico
6. Skullcap
7. Brick carrier
8. Vomiting
9. Double curve
10. Evil
11. Indigo
19. Sunbeam
21. In the direction of
22. Rocky tableland
23. Adjoin
24. Not any
25. Rotational speed
27. U-turn (Colloq)
28. Suburb of Cairo
29. As previously given
30. Prefix, distant
32. Chop
33. Pertaining to the Sudan
35. Mooing
36. Paddle
37. Therefore
38. Pulpy
39. Dutch cheese
40. Row
41. Wagers
42. Mast
45. Cattle low
47. Island (France)
48. Relation
49. Consume

solution 36

G	O	B	I		B	L	U	R		Q E D

(Grid solution:)

Row 1: G O B I ■ B L U R ■ Q E D
Row 2: N A I L ■ E A S E ■ U T E
Row 3: U R G E ■ G R A B ■ A T E
Row 4: ■ ■ ■ I C E D ■ A U G E R
Row 5: A D Y T U M ■ I T S ■ ■ ■
Row 6: C H O I R ■ A L E ■ B E T
Row 7: M A R S ■ A R K ■ H I D E
Row 8: E L K ■ B I C ■ P A N D A
Row 9: ■ ■ ■ N E D ■ S E L D O M
Row 10: J A B O T ■ F U R Y ■ ■ ■
Row 11: O L E ■ T A R T ■ A L I T
Row 12: S E N ■ O D E R ■ R A C E
Row 13: H E T ■ R O T A ■ D Y E D

ACROSS
1. Mongolian desert
5. Make indistinct
9. Which was to be proved
12. Metal spike
13. Relax
14. Small truck
15. Incite
16. Clutch
17. Dined
18. Decorated cake
20. Tool for boring holes
22. Sacred shrine
25. Sexless things
26. Singing group
27. Beer
28. Wager
31. Red planet
32. Noah's vessel
33. Conceal
34. Moose
35. Ballpoint biro
36. Black and white Chinese animal
37. - Kelly
38. Not very often
39. Ruffle
42. Rage
43. Bullfight call
44. Pastry item
46. Got down from mount
50. Monetary unit of Japan
51. River in central Europe
52. Sprint contest
53. - up, excited
54. Roster
55. Changed colour of

DOWN
1. Wildebeest
2. Paddle
3. Large
4. Inflammation of the ileum
5. Adorn with precious stones
6. Fat
7. America (Abbr)
8. Discount
9. Quagmire
10. Suffix, diminutive
11. Antlered beast
19. Worthless dog
21. Objective case of we
22. Pinnacle
23. Indian pulses
24. Royal House
25. Family
27. Part of a circle
28. Tie
29. Root of the taro
30. Side
32. Assist
33. Line for hoisting a sail
35. Person who bets
36. Each
37. Negative vote
38. Hindu scripture
39. Good-natured banter
40. To the sheltered side
41. Crooked
42. Worry
45. Fuss
47. Secular
48. Freeze
49. Spread out for drying

solution 37

L	A	G	S		T	R	I	M		S	E	E
E	D	A	M		R	A	L	E		E	L	M
E	D	D	O		I	S	L	E		E	L	I
			L	A	T	H		T	O	P	E	R
P	A	D	D	L	E		E	L	F			
S	C	R	E	E		H	O	Y		S	O	T
S	E	A	R		V	I	N		S	L	O	B
T	R	Y		M	A	D		B	A	I	Z	A
		S	U	N		W	I	N	T	E	R	
I	D	I	O	M		A	I	N	T			
R	E	D		M	E	S	S		A	H	O	Y
E	E	L		E	R	I	E		F	E	R	E
S	P	Y		R	E	A	R		E	N	D	S

ACROSS
1. Delays
5. Decorate (Xmas tree)
9. Witness
12. Dutch cheese
13. Death rattle
14. Shady tree
15. Root of the taro
16. Small island
17. Biblical high priest
18. Slat
20. Heavy drinker
22. Oar
25. Fairy
26. Gravelly hillside
27. Bingo-like game
28. Drunkard
31. Scorch
32. Wine
33. Untidy person
34. Attempt
35. Insane
36. Monetary unit of Oman
37. Sol
38. Cold season
39. Jargon
42. Isn't
43. Colour
44. Untidy state
46. Nautical call
50. Conger
51. A Great Lake
52. Comrade
53. Secret agent
54. Back
55. Finishes

DOWN
1. Sheltered side
2. Sum
3. Goad for driving cattle
4. Burn without flame
5. Banal
6. Hasty
7. Sick
8. Fittingly
9. Ooze
10. Australian super-model
11. Islamic chieftain
19. Beer
21. Belonging to
22. Surreptitious, attention getting sound
23. The maple
24. Cart
25. An age
27. Concealed
28. Narrow aperture
29. Seep
30. Type of automatic gear selector (1-3)
32. Forefront
33. Capital of New Mexico
35. Pantomimist
36. Garbage can
37. Therefore
38. More sensible
39. Angers
40. Profound
41. Lazily
42. Largest continent
45. Before
47. Female bird
48. W.A. river
49. Affirmative response

solution 38

R	E	E	D		H	A	U	T		K	O	I
O	G	E	E		U	L	N	A		U	P	S
B	O	L	A		L	O	I	N		D	A	L
			L	U	K	E		D	H	O	L	E
C	O	W	E	R	S		L	E	E			
A	D	O	R	N		C	A	M		D	Y	E
K	E	O	S		B	O	Y		B	E	E	R
E	R	S		D	E	B		H	E	E	L	S
			S	O	L		P	A	D	D	L	E
A	L	T	O	S		E	A	S	T			
P	I	E		A	R	T	S		I	M	P	S
S	E	A		G	E	T	S		M	U	S	E
E	F	T		E	P	E	E		E	D	I	T

ACROSS
1. Marsh plant
5. High-class
9. Colorful form of the common carp
12. Double curve
13. Arm bone
14. Raises
15. South American weapon
16. Meat cut
17. Indian dish
18. One of the Disciples
20. Wild Asian dog
22. Shrinks from
25. Sheltered side
26. Decorate
27. Eccentric wheel
28. Change colour of
31. Greek island in the Aegean
32. Lad
33. Ale
34. Bitter vetch
35. Debutante
36. Feet parts
37. The sun
38. Oar
39. Singers
42. The Orient
43. Pastry item
44. Non-scientific studies
46. Little devils
50. Large body of water
51. Obtains
52. Ponder
53. Newt
54. Fencing sword
55. Redact

DOWN
1. Hold up
2. The self
3. Conger
4. Traders
5. Bodies of ruined ships
6. Agave
7. Prefix, one
8. Bicycle for two
9. Accolade
10. Iridescent gem
11. Small island
19. Vase
21. Masculine pronoun
22. Shaped mass of food
23. River in central Europe
24. Courts
25. Secular
27. Corn ear
28. Property title
29. Shout
30. Gaelic
32. Unit of loudness
33. The time a person goes to bed
35. Prescribed quantity of medicine
36. Owns
37. Therefore
38. Out of date
39. Church recess
40. Willing
41. Nipple
42. Suffix, diminutive
45. Corded fabric
47. Mire
48. Pressure symbol
49. Become firm

solution 39

L	I	M	A		D	Y	A	K		C	A	N
A	L	A	R		A	E	R	O		L	A	E
X	E	N	O		V	A	M	P		O	R	E
			U	S	E	S		E	I	D	E	R
L	O	O	S	E	N		A	C	T			
O	L	D	E	N		A	R	K		W	A	R
V	I	E	D		E	F	T		D	E	L	E
E	O	S		S	E	T		T	A	P	E	D
			B	E	L		P	O	S	T	E	D
B	A	B	E	L		A	E	R	Y			
O	P	E		D	I	S	C		U	P	O	N
N	I	N		O	C	T	A		R	A	L	E
G	A	S		M	E	I	N		E	D	D	O

ACROSS
1. Peruvian capital
5. Aborigine of Borneo
9. Is able to
12. Having wings
13. Prefix, air
14. New Guinea seaport
15. Prefix, foreign
16. Adventuress
17. Crude mineral
18. Employs
20. Downy duck
22. Slacken
25. Play division
26. Ancient
27. Noah's vessel
28. Battle
31. Competed
32. Newt
33. Delete (Printing)
34. Greek goddess of the dawn
35. Become firm
36. Bandaged
37. Unit of loudness
38. Mailed
39. Confused mixture of sounds
42. Ethereal
43. Open
44. Circular plate
46. On top of
50. A fool
51. Prefix, eight
52. Death rattle
53. Vapour
54. Hitler's autobiography, "-Kampf"
55. Root of the taro

DOWN
1. Slack
2. Island (France)
3. Human race
4. Stirred
5. Recite the Jewish prayers
6. Shouts of agreement
7. Limb
8. Currency unit of the Soviet Union
9. Lump of clay
10. River in central Switzerland
11. Never
19. Monetary unit of Japan
21. Neuter singular pronoun
22. Adore
23. Potpourri
24. Poems
25. Talent
27. Nautical, rear
28. Sobbed
29. To the sheltered side
30. Spawning area of salmon
32. Conger
33. Carnivorous marsupial
35. Not very often
36. Rocky peak
37. To exist
38. Hickory nut
39. Dull resonant sound
40. Capital of Western Samoa
41. Scottish hills
42. Italian wine province
45. Freeze
47. Cushion
48. Aged
49. Prefix, new

solution 40

C	U	F	F		B	L	O	W		L	O	N
A	S	E	A		R	A	V	E		A	X	E
B	A	W	L		O	V	A	L		M	E	S
			S	I	N	E		K	H	A	N	S
S	Y	R	I	N	X		T	I	E			
W	A	I	T	S		B	A	N		C	U	D
A	L	L	Y		C	U	E		V	I	S	A
B	E	E		T	O	D		F	E	A	S	T
			B	O	O		F	E	D	O	R	A
A	D	I	E	U		O	O	Z	E			
P	A	R		P	I	N	S		T	O	K	E
E	R	A		E	V	E	S		T	H	O	R
D	E	N		E	Y	R	A		E	M	I	R

ACROSS
1. Wristband
5. Gust
9. Actor, - Chaney
12. At sea
13. Rant
14. Chop
15. Howl
16. Egg-shaped
17. My, French (Plural)
18. Trigonometric function
20. Persian lords
22. Vocal organ of birds
25. Bind
26. Delays
27. Prohibit
28. Rumen
31. Friend
32. Prompt
33. Entry permit
34. Hive insect
35. Fox
36. Repast
37. Jeer
38. Trilby hat
39. Farewell
42. Seep
43. Normal
44. Dowels
46. Gratuity
50. An age
51. Days before
52. Norse god of thunder
53. Lair
54. Jaguarundi
55. Islamic chieftain

DOWN
1. Taxi
2. America (Abbr)
3. Not many
4. Treachery
5. New York city borough
6. Wash
7. Eggs
8. The vault of heaven
9. Tibetan monk
10. Beasts of burden
11. Scottish headland
19. - and outs, intricacies
21. Masculine pronoun
22. Mop
23. American university
24. Anger
25. - kwon do (Korean martial art)
27. Immature flower
28. Goodbye
29. Former Soviet Union
30. Information
32. Dove's call
33. Mounted sentry
35. Wig
36. Turkish cap
37. To exist
38. Cavity
39. Mimicked
40. Challenge
41. Republic in SW Asia
42. Unique thing
45. Climbing plant
47. Electrical resistance unit
48. Colorful form of the common carp
49. Go wrong

solution 41

S	N	U	G	■	I	D	O	L	■	L	A	M
E	A	R	L	■	L	I	N	E	■	A	L	E
N	E	N	E	■	E	G	O	S	■	V	E	E
■	■	■	E	Y	A	S	■	S	M	A	C	K
U	N	I	F	I	C	■	P	O	E	■	■	■
R	E	R	U	N	■	C	A	R	■	B	I	T
T	O	O	L	■	B	O	Y	■	T	O	S	H
I	N	N	■	S	A	Y	■	C	E	L	L	O
■	■	■	G	O	T	■	B	O	L	D	E	R
N	A	B	O	B	■	M	E	W	S	■	■	■
O	A	R	■	E	M	I	R	■	T	I	E	D
A	R	E	■	R	U	D	E	■	A	L	L	Y
H	E	N	■	S	M	I	T	■	R	E	D	E

ACROSS
1. Cosy
5. Object of worship
9. Thrash
12. Nobleman
13. Row
14. Beer
15. Hawaiian goose
16. Personalities
17. Victory sign
18. Nestling
20. Hit
22. Causing unity
25. "The Raven" author
26. Television repeat
27. Automobile
28. Piece
31. Implement
32. Lad
33. Nonsense
34. Tavern
35. Utter
36. Large violin-like instrument
37. Obtained
38. More daring
39. Wealthy person
42. Street of stabling
43. Paddle
44. Islamic chieftain
46. Bound
50. Land measure
51. Uncivil
52. Friend
53. Female bird
54. Struck
55. Advise

DOWN
1. Monetary unit of Japan
2. Not
3. Vase
4. Merry
5. Pertaining to the ileum
6. Excavates
7. Yoko -
8. Person who grants a lease
9. Molten rock
10. Smart - , show-off
11. Humble
19. - and Yang
21. Objective case of I
22. Upper respiratory tract infection
23. Lighting gas
24. Press clothes
25. Wages
27. Bashful
28. Daring
29. Small island
30. Norse god of thunder
32. Flying mammal
33. Communications satellite
35. Sir Garfield -, West Indian cricketer
36. Bovine
37. Depart
38. Tam
39. Ark builder
40. River in central Switzerland
41. Machine-gun
42. Skirt coming to just below knee
45. Mother
47. Island (France)
48. Antiquity
49. Change colour of

solution 42

N	A	R	C		O	B	E	Y		I	N	S
I	L	I	A		V	E	G	A		L	A	E
P	E	G	S		A	E	O	N		I	R	E
			C	A	L	F		Q	U	A	C	K
C	E	D	A	R	S		J	U	S			
A	B	O	D	E		L	E	I		T	O	G
N	O	N	E		L	E	T		T	I	N	E
T	N	T		L	E	U		D	A	L	E	S
			P	I	N		M	O	D	E	S	T
A	E	G	I	S		B	E	E	P			
C	A	N		S	H	I	N		O	N	L	Y
I	S	A		O	O	P	S		L	A	S	E
D	E	R		M	E	S	A		E	N	D	S

ACROSS
1. Narcotics agent
5. Heed
9. - and outs, intricacies
12. Hip bones
13. Star in Lyra
14. New Guinea seaport
15. Clothesline clips
16. Great age
17. Anger
18. Young cow
20. Sound of a duck
22. Timber trees
25. Legal right
26. Dwelling
27. Garland
28. To clothe
31. Not any
32. Allow
33. Prong
34. An explosive
35. Monetary unit of Romania
36. Valleys
37. Transfix
38. Demure
39. Sponsorship
42. High-pitched tone
43. Is able to
44. Leg part
46. Merely
50. Mount - , N.W. Qld. mining town
51. Expression used when accident happens
52. Cut with laser
53. The (German)
54. Rocky tableland
55. Finishes

DOWN
1. Pinch
2. Beer
3. Outfit
4. Waterfall
5. Sportsgrounds
6. Cow flesh
7. The self
8. Yankee
9. Hip bones
10. Narcotics agent
11. Search for
19. Land measure
21. Objective case of we
22. Tilt
23. Black
24. Do not
25. Black
27. Monetary unit of Romania
28. Roofing slate
29. Single items
30. Romance tale
32. Pet form of Leonard
33. Young frog
35. Limber, supple
36. Female deer
37. The ratio between circumference and diameter
38. Altar stone
39. Etching fluid
40. Relax
41. Growl
42. Beeps horn
45. Gardening tool
47. Grandmother
48. Hallucinogenic drug
49. Affirmative response

solution 43

C	A	V	E	■	S	E	R	E	■	S	P	A
U	R	E	A	■	U	P	O	N	■	O	R	B
B	E	T	S	■	D	E	B	S	■	Y	O	B
■	■	■	E	A	S	E	■	U	S	A	G	E
M	A	Y	F	L	Y	■	G	E	O	■	■	■
A	F	O	U	L	■	P	A	D	■	B	E	T
M	A	L	L	■	C	U	B	■	S	U	R	A
A	R	K	■	C	A	B	■	T	U	R	N	S
■	■	■	D	A	M	■	S	A	B	R	E	S
D	E	C	O	Y	■	A	L	I	T	■	■	■
I	S	A	■	M	O	V	E	■	E	R	N	S
P	A	S	■	A	L	O	W	■	N	E	A	P
S	U	E	■	N	E	W	S	■	D	E	N	Y

ACROSS
1. Grotto
5. Withered
9. Mineral spring
12. Fertiliser
13. On top of
14. Sphere
15. Wagers
16. Debutantes
17. Teenage lout
18. Relax
20. Consumption
22. Ephemerid
25. Prefix, the earth
26. In an entangled state
27. Cushion
28. Wager
31. Shopping centre
32. Young bear
33. Chapter of the Koran
34. Noah's vessel
35. Taxi
36. Revolves
37. Weir
38. Cavalry sword
39. Lure
42. Got down from mount
43. Mount - , N.W. Qld. mining town
44. Budge
46. Sea eagles
50. Dance step
51. Nautical, below
52. Lowest high tide
53. Take to court
54. Tidings
55. Refuse

DOWN
1. Young bear
2. Land measure
3. Examine thoroughly
4. Soothing
5. Resembling suds
6. Fencing sword
7. Hold up
8. Followed
9. Soybean
10. Forage
11. French clergyman
19. Everything
21. Therefore
22. Mother
23. Distant
24. Egg part
25. Talk
27. Hotel
28. Bindi-eye prickle
29. Sea eagle
30. Soviet news service
32. Eccentric wheel
33. Occur beneath
35. Alligator
36. - Chi. Slow moving martial art form
37. Perform
38. Swings to the side
39. Immerses
40. Son of Isaac and Rebekah
41. Instance
42. Confess
45. Bullfight call
47. Female ruff
48. Grandmother
49. Secret agent

solution 44

G	R	O	G	■	I	W	I	S	■	G	I	G
A	O	N	E	■	S	A	C	K	■	O	B	I
B	O	E	R	■	A	R	E	A	■	B	E	L
■	■	■	M	A	A	M	■	T	W	I	X	T
J	U	D	A	I	C	■	Z	E	E	■	■	■
E	L	A	N	D	■	F	O	R	■	G	U	N
A	N	T	E	■	P	R	O	■	T	A	R	O
N	A	E	■	P	R	O	■	A	E	G	I	S
■	■	■	P	L	Y	■	E	N	L	A	C	E
T	I	B	I	A	■	A	D	D	S	■	■	■
A	D	O	■	S	U	N	G	■	T	O	O	K
U	L	T	■	M	E	T	E	■	A	C	R	E
T	E	A	■	A	Y	E	S	■	R	H	E	A

ACROSS
1. Beer (Colloq)
5. Certainly
9. Sulky
12. First class (1-3)
13. Bag
14. Japanese sash
15. South African
16. Region
17. Unit of loudness
18. Madam
20. Betwixt
22. Jewish
25. Letter Z
26. African antelope
27. In favour of
28. Firearm
31. Poker stake
32. In favour of
33. Polynesian root food
34. Not
35. In favour of
36. Sponsorship
37. 3 Thickness
38. Entwine
39. Shinbone
42. Appends
43. Fuss
44. Carolled
46. Captured
50. Last month
51. Measure out
52. Land measure
53. An infusion
54. Affirmative votes
55. Ostrich-like bird

DOWN
1. Talk
2. Kangaroo
3. Monad
4. Relevant
5. Son of Abraham
6. Fairly hot
7. Freeze
8. Performer on ice
9. Mongolian desert
10. Mountain goat
11. Golden
19. Assist
21. Plural of I
22. Sturdy twilled fabric
23. Arm bone
24. An appointment
25. Menagerie
27. To and -
28. Insane
29. Of urine
30. Proboscis
32. Snoop
33. Communications satellite
35. Blood fluid
36. Also
37. The ratio between circumference and diameter
38. Borders
39. Tense
40. Lazy
41. Goatskin bag for holding wine
42. Poker stake
45. U-turn (Colloq)
47. Scottish expression
48. Crude mineral
49. New Zealand parrot

solution 45

Y	A	N	G		B	O	T	A		B	A	T
A	L	O	E		U	N	I	T		E	G	O
H	E	N	S		R	E	L	Y		R	O	E
			T	A	R	S		P	I	N	G	S
Q	U	E	A	N	S		P	I	N			
U	N	I	T	Y		S	E	C		B	U	T
A	C	R	E		S	I	R		L	A	S	E
D	O	E		Y	E	S		P	O	K	E	R
		T	E	A		A	U	B	U	R	N	
C	H	A	O	S		E	E	L	S			
O	O	H		M	E	M	O		T	I	R	E
O	N	O		A	K	I	N		E	D	I	T
K	E	Y		N	E	T	S		R	A	G	A

ACROSS
1. Yin and -
5. Goatskin bag for holding wine
9. Flying mammal
12. Agave
13. Military detachment
14. The self
15. Female birds
16. Depend
17. Fish eggs
18. Sailors
20. Sharp ringing sounds
22. Shrews
25. Transfix
26. Oneness
27. Dry (wine)
28. However
31. Land measure
32. Knight's title
33. Cut with laser
34. Female deer
35. Affirmative response
36. Card game
37. An infusion
38. Reddish-brown hair
39. Disorder
42. Long fish
43. Exclamation of wonder
44. Brief note
46. Weary
50. Yoko -
51. Related
52. Redact
53. Unlocking implement
54. Devices for fishing
55. Hindu music

DOWN
1. Exclamation of disgust
2. Beer
3. Prefix, not
4. Develop slowly
5. Bindi-eye prickles
6. Single items
7. Sesame plant
8. Abnormal
9. Capital of Switzerland
10. Eager
11. Pedal digits
19. Some
21. Prefix meaning not
22. Quadrangle
23. Remarkable
24. Ireland
25. Each
27. Sister
28. Capital of Azerbaijan
29. Consumer
30. Sea bird
32. Large body of water
33. Marine crustacean
35. Sycophant
36. Monetary unit of Afghanistan
37. In the direction of
38. Ages
39. Prepare food
40. Sharpen
41. Nautical call
42. Send out
45. Supplement existence
47. Highest mountain in Crete
48. Outfit
49. Greek letter

solution 46

P	A	C	T		C	R	A	B		V	A	N
O	N	E	R		R	A	G	A		E	G	O
E	T	T	E		A	N	E	W		I	O	U
			N	A	Z	I		B	U	N	G	S
P	E	D	D	L	E		Y	E	P			
S	L	E	E	T		W	E	E		L	E	U
S	L	E	D		B	A	A		B	E	D	S
T	E	D		F	O	X		C	R	A	G	S
		B	O	Y		W	E	E	D	E	R	
F	I	V	E	R		P	A	P	A			
O	N	E		G	O	L	F		D	O	H	S
I	C	E		E	P	E	E		T	H	A	I
L	A	P		D	E	A	R		H	O	D	S

ACROSS
1. Agreement
5. Crustacean
9. Forefront
12. Unique thing
13. Hindu music
14. The self
15. Suffix, diminutive
16. Once again
17. Acknowledgement of debt
18. Follower of Hitler
20. Stoppers
22. Hawk goods
25. Yes
26. Rain and snow
27. Tiny
28. Monetary unit of Romania
31. Toboggan
32. Bleat
33. Cots
34. Spread out for drying
35. Sly animal
36. Rocky heights
37. Lad
38. Gardening tool
39. Five pound note
42. Father
43. Monad
44. Greg Norman's sport
46. Notes at scale's ends
50. Freeze
51. Fencing sword
52. Siamese
53. Fold
54. Precious
55. Brick carriers

DOWN
1. "The Raven" author
2. Social insect
3. Prefix, whale
4. Tended
5. Derange
6. Indian queen
7. Mature
8. Old Scottish bullion coin
9. Streak of ore
10. Eager
11. Commonsense
19. High-pitched
21. Toward the top
22. Surreptitious, attention getting sound
23. Australian super-model
24. Property title
25. Yes
27. Bee product
28. Heavy metal
29. Brink
30. Former Soviet Union
32. Lad
33. Width
35. Counterfeited
36. Brown-capped boletus mushroom
37. To exist
38. A sacrament
39. Thwart
40. Ancient Peruvian
41. Vice president
42. Prayer
45. Open
47. Exclamation of surprise
48. Possessed
49. Sister

solution 47

R	I	P	E	■	L	W	E	I	B	O	T
A	C	E	D	■	A	E	R	O	■	O	B	S
Y	E	T	I	■	R	E	E	D	■	M	O	A
■	■	■	T	A	C	K	■	O	M	B	E	R
P	A	R	I	S	H	■	R	U	E	■	■	■
S	C	O	O	P	■	C	O	S	■	G	I	B
S	H	U	N	■	M	A	Y	■	J	A	D	E
T	E	T	■	T	A	N	■	M	O	O	L	A
■	■	■	S	O	N	■	F	A	B	L	E	D
G	A	L	O	P	■	O	U	C	H	■	■	■
R	O	O	■	P	I	R	N	■	U	R	T	I
I	N	S	■	E	L	A	N	■	N	O	E	L
N	E	E	■	R	E	L	Y	■	T	E	A	K

ACROSS
1. Mature
5. Monetary unit of Angola
9. Fly larva
12. Beaten by tennis service
13. Prefix, air
14. Observation
15. Abominable snowman
16. Marsh plant
17. New Zealand bird
18. Small nail
20. Card game for three
22. Diocese
25. Regret
26. Ladle
27. Long-leaved lettuce
28. Castrated male cat
31. Avoid
32. A month
33. Green stone
34. 9th letter of the Hebrew alphabet
35. Brown shade
36. Money
37. Male offspring
38. Renowned
39. Lively dance
42. Ornamental brooch
43. Kangaroo
44. Fishing reel
46. Upper respiratory tract infection
50. - and outs, intricacies
51. Dash
52. Christmas
53. Born
54. Depend
55. Timber tree

DOWN
1. Sunbeam
2. Freeze
3. Domesticated animal
4. Particular printing of book
5. Coniferous tree
6. Seven days
7. Before
8. Pertaining to iodine
9. Explosive device
10. Hautboy
11. Russian emperor
19. Egyptian serpent
21. Objective case of I
22. Surreptitious, attention getting sound
23. Pain
24. Disorderly flight
25. - Rene. Mo
27. Is able to
28. Jail
29. Lazy
30. Necklace component
32. Human race
33. Seek employment
35. Top hat
36. Raincoat
37. Therefore
38. Amusing
39. Smile
40. First class (1-3)
41. Be defeated
42. Spoken
45. Island (France)
47. Fish eggs
48. An infusion
49. Family

solution 48

H	U	M	P		U	M	B	O		H	U	B
A	S	E	A		S	E	E	K		A	G	E
Y	A	N	G		N	I	N	A		I	L	E
			E	D	E	N		P	O	L	Y	P
R	A	M	A	D	A		P	I	N			
A	G	E	N	T		G	A	S		L	S	D
G	E	N	T		B	I	T		S	I	L	O
A	D	D		J	I	B		R	H	E	U	M
		D	U	O		C	H	A	S	E	S	
N	A	B	O	B		F	O	O	D			
E	W	E		B	U	R	R		I	N	F	O
A	R	T		A	Z	A	N		E	A	R	P
R	Y	A		H	I	P	S		R	Y	O	T

ACROSS
1. Mound
5. Boss on a shield
9. Nave
12. At sea
13. Search for
14. Mature
15. Yin and -
16. One of Columbus's ships
17. Island (France)
18. Paradise
20. Coral builder
22. Open shelter
25. Transfix
26. Spy
27. Vapour
28. Hallucinogenic drug
31. A man
32. Piece
33. Grain store
34. Sum
35. Crane boom
36. A cold
37. Twosome
38. Pursues
39. Wealthy person
42. Nourishment
43. Female sheep
44. Bindi-eye prickle
46. Information
50. Talent
51. Islamic call to prayer
52. Wyatt -
53. Handwoven Scandinavian rug
54. Coxae
55. Indian peasant

DOWN
1. Cattle fodder
2. America (Abbr)
3. Soldiers
4. Spectacle
5. Pale green mosslike lichen
6. Hitler's autobiography, "- Kampf"
7. Scottish hill
8. Giraffe-like animals
9. Greet
10. Unattractive
11. High-pitched tone
19. Once common, now banned, insecticide
21. Not off
22. Hindu music
23. Old
24. Repair
25. Dab
27. Castrated male cat
28. Falsehoods
29. Swing around
30. Benedictine monks' titles
32. Prefix, life
33. More protected from sun
35. Moslem robe
36. 17th letter of the Greek alphabet
37. Perform
38. Cures with brine
39. Close to
40. Askew
41. Greek letter
42. Bind securely (Nautical)
45. Israeli submachine gun
47. No
48. To and -
49. Choose

solution 49

D	R	A	G		H	O	O	K		S	E	T
O	H	I	O		A	B	B	E		U	S	E
R	O	D	S		P	E	S	T		L	A	E
			L	I	L	Y		O	A	K	U	M
P	A	C	I	F	Y		A	S	S			
I	C	O	N	S		R	Y	E		L	E	U
P	R	I	G		A	P	E		S	O	T	S
S	E	N		R	P	M		K	N	O	T	S
		G	U	T		L	O	O	P	E	R	
K	L	O	O	F		B	E	A	R			
I	O	N		O	S	L	O		T	B	A	R
T	R	Y		U	P	O	N		E	A	S	E
S	E	X		S	Y	C	E		D	Y	K	E

ACROSS
1. Haul
5. Crook
9. Become firm
12. U.S. State
13. French clergyman
14. Avail of
15. Staffs
16. Nuisance
17. New Guinea seaport
18. Bulb flower
20. Loose fiber used for caulking
22. Appease
25. Donkey
26. Images
27. Cereal
28. Monetary unit of Romania
31. Prude
32. Primate
33. Drunkards
34. Monetary unit of Japan
35. Rotational speed
36. Ravels
37. Remove intestines from fish
38. Inchworm
39. Ravine
42. Ursa
43. Charged particle
44. Capital of Norway
46. Type of automatic gear selector (1-3)
50. Attempt
51. On top of
52. Relax
53. Gender
54. Stable attendant
55. Levee

DOWN
1. Beetle
2. 17th letter of the Greek alphabet
3. Assist
4. Young goose
5. Perhaps
6. Heed
7. Observation
8. Monosaccharide
9. Peevish fit
10. Son of Isaac and Rebekah
11. Abound
19. Possibilities
21. Similar to
22. Fruit seeds
23. Land measure
24. Piece of money
25. Affirmative vote
27. Rotational speed
28. Noose
29. Suffix, diminutive
30. Former Soviet Union
32. Fitting
33. Grunted
35. Tinged with red
36. Hawaiian acacia
37. Depart
38. Monetary unit of Sierra Leone
39. Packs
40. Tradition
41. Variety of chalcedony
42. Political combine
45. Secret agent
47. Cove
48. Question
49. Female ruff

solution 50

R	A	K	E		A	M	E	N		S	H	E
O	P	E	C		L	E	T	O		O	A	T
T	E	A	L		T	O	A	D		L	I	T
			A	R	O	W		D	H	O	L	E
P	O	K	I	E	S		R	E	E			
L	I	A	R	D		R	I	D		D	A	B
E	L	L	S		P	I	P		R	U	B	E
B	Y	E		R	U	B		M	I	M	E	D
			D	U	B		G	A	B	B	L	E
C	H	A	O	S		P	O	L	K			
O	O	H		T	O	L	D		N	I	G	H
B	O	O		E	P	E	E		I	D	E	A
S	K	Y		D	E	B	T		T	O	T	O

ACROSS
1. Garden tool
5. Prayer ending
9. That woman
12. Oil cartel
13. Mother of Apollo
14. Breakfast cereal
15. Freshwater duck
16. Amphibian
17. Ignited
18. In a line
20. Wild Asian dog
22. One-armed bandits (Colloq)
25. Female ruff
26. River in W Canada
27. Free
28. Skilled
31. Old cloth measures
32. Fruit seed
33. Hick
34. Farewell
35. Chafe
36. Acted silently
37. Name
38. Jabber
39. Disorder
42. 11th president of the U.S
43. Exclamation of wonder
44. Informed
46. Near
50. Jeer
51. Fencing sword
52. Notion
53. Firmament
54. Something owing
55. In -, in all

DOWN
1. Decay
2. Primate
3. New Zealand parrot
4. Chocolate and cream delicacies
5. Singers
6. Sound of a cat
7. Greek letter
8. Inclined head
9. Performance by one
10. Greet
11. Suffix, diminutive
19. Colour
21. Masculine pronoun
22. Plebeian
23. Greasy
24. Cabbagelike plant
25. Tear
27. Chest bone
28. Mute
29. Cain's victim
30. English monk
32. Hotel
33. Knitted pattern
35. Oxidised
36. - de mer, seasickness
37. Perform
38. Triangular insert
39. Male swans
40. Crook
41. Nautical call
42. Plebeian
45. Open
47. Revised form of Esperanto
48. Obtain
49. Monetary unit of Vietnam

solution 51

	A	M		G	A	I	L	Y	
U	N	R	E	E	L	S		I	N
R		S	A	L	T		A	D	O
A	T		U	S		A	N	D	
T	O	E				S	T	I	R
E	U	R	O			A	S	H	
	C	A	R		U	P		H	E
G	A	S		T	S	A	R		A
O	N		P	O	S	S	E	S	S
	S	P	I	E	R		D	O	

ACROSS
1. Part of the verb "to be"
3. Merrily
7. Unwinds
9. Prefix meaning not
11. Seasoning
12. Fuss
13. Near to
15. Objective case of we
16. Also
17. Pedal digit
19. Agitate
21. Wallaroo
23. Fire remains
24. Automobile
25. Toward the top
27. Masculine pronoun
28. Vapour
29. Russian emperor
31. Not off
32. Own
34. Watcher
35. Perform

DOWN
1. Prefix meaning without
2. Missus
3. Sets
4. High-pitched
5. Part of the verb to be
6. Language of European Jews
7. Salt of uric acid
8. French, water
10. Negative vote
12. Rectangular pier
14. Enormously-beaked tropical American birds
16. Similar to
18. Periods of history
20. Ostrich-like birds
22. Otherwise
25. Former Soviet Union
26. Dance step
28. Depart
29. Pedal digit
30. Colour
32. The ratio between circumference and diameter
33. Therefore

solution 52

	O	N		L	A	B	A	N	
U	K	U	L	E	L	E		U	S
T		B	A	T	E		I	D	O
I	N		D	O		H	O	G	
L	E	A				I	W	I	S
E	L	L	S				A	N	I
	S	A	O		G	O		G	O
T	O	R		F	L	U	B		U
O	N		B	E	A	T	R	I	X
	S	P	E	N	D		A	N	

ACROSS
1. Not off
3. Father of Leah and Rachel
7. Stringed instrument
9. Objective case of we
11. Restrain
12. Revised form of Esperanto
13. Prefix meaning not
15. Perform
16. Pig
17. Meadow
19. Certainly
21. Old cloth measures
23. Black bird
24. Cracker biscuit
25. Depart
27. Depart
28. Rocky peak
29. Bungle
31. Not off
32. Netherlands queen
34. Outlay
35. Prefix meaning without

DOWN
1. Satisfactory
2. Gist
3. Mother of Apollo
4. Beer
5. To exist
6. Elbowing
7. Useful
8. Boy
10. Therefore
12. U.S. State
14. Wrestling holds
16. Hello there
18. Having wings
20. American Indian
22. Therefore
25. Pleased
26. Not at home
28. In the direction of
29. Marsh
30. Brassiere
32. To exist
33. Prefix meaning not

solution 53

	O	F		S	M	O	K	Y	
S	K	E	E	T	E	R		A	N
L		N	A	O	S		R	H	O
U	S		U	P		T	O	W	
E	W	E				O	M	I	T
D	E	L	I			P	S	I	
	A	L	T		O	N		M	E
A	T	E		A	R	O	W		R
M	E		D	O	G	T	A	G	S
	R	O	O	K	Y		S	O	

ACROSS
1. Belonging to
3. Hazy
7. Mosquito (Colloq)
9. Prefix meaning without
11. Temple
12. 17th letter of the Greek alphabet
13. Objective case of we
15. Toward the top
16. Haul
17. Female sheep
19. Exclude
21. Delicatessen
23. Pressure symbol
24. High-pitched
25. Not off
27. Objective case of I
28. Dined
29. In a line
31. Objective case of I
32. Identity discs (3.4)
34. Frequented by rooks
35. Therefore

DOWN
1. Satisfactory
2. Marsh
3. Halt
4. My, French (Plural)
5. Otherwise
6. Worship of Yahweh
7. Veered
8. French, water
10. Negative vote
12. Gambol
14. Knitted jacket
16. In the direction of
18. Australian super-model
20. Rows
22. Neuter singular pronoun
25. Wild revelry
26. Negating word
28. Part of the verb "to be"
29. Very good (1-2)
30. Once existed
32. Perform
33. Depart

solution 54

	M	E		K	O	A	L	A
L	Y	N	C	E	A	N		G	O
O		D	I	N	K		V	I	N
T		D	O		S	I	T	
I	D	E			O	V	A	L
C	O	R	N			A	T	E
	R	I	O		W	E		O	X
H	A	N		M	O	L	D		I
I	N		P	A	R	I	A	H	S
	T	H	I	C	K		B	E

ACROSS
1. Objective case of I
3. Australian marsupial
7. Sharp-sighted
9. Depart
11. Double on a bicycle (Colloq)
12. Wine
13. In the direction of
15. Perform
16. Take a seat
17. Carp-like fish
19. Egg-shaped
21. Maize
23. Dined
24. - de Janeiro
25. Plural of I
27. Bovine beast
28. A dynasty in China
29. Shape
31. Prefix meaning not
32. Social outcasts
34. Dense
35. To exist

DOWN
1. Possessive form of me
2. Finish
3. Lotto-like gambling game
4. Large tree
5. Prefix meaning without
6. Restless (music)
7. Living in flowing water
8. Spanish hero
10. Not off
12. Exclamation of acclaim
14. Odorous substance
16. Therefore
18. Ireland
20. Lexicon
22. Negative vote
25. Toil
26. Biblical high priest
28. Hello there
29. Raincoat
30. Skilled
32. The ratio between circumference and diameter
33. Masculine pronoun

solution 55

	A	M		M	A	H	D	I	
A	N	A	G	O	G	E		N	O
H		Y	O	K	O		A	S	K
O	F		B	E		A	M	U	
Y	A	K				S	E	R	B
S	L	A	M			N	E	O	
	S	K	Y		D	O		D	O
T	I	A		P	O	U	R		K
O	F		A	S	H	R	A	M	S
	Y	E	T	I	S		W	E	

ACROSS
1. Part of the verb "to be"
3. Muslim messiah
7. Spiritual interpretation
9. Negative vote
11. - Ono
12. Question
13. Belonging to
15. To exist
16. Atomic mass unit
17. Tibetan ox
19. Yugoslavian
21. Close hard
23. Prefix, new
24. Firmament
25. Perform
27. Perform
28. - Maria, coffee liqueur
29. Decant
31. Belonging to
32. Hindu religious retreats
34. Abominable snowmen
35. Plural of I

DOWN
1. Prefix meaning without
2. A month
3. Donkey
4. In the past
5. Masculine pronoun
6. Made sure
7. Nautical calls
8. Sailor
10. Satisfactory
12. Prayer ending
14. Fraudulently alter
16. Similar to
18. New Zealand parrot
20. Volumes
22. Possessive form of me
25. Notes at scale's ends
26. Of us
28. In the direction of
29. Pressure symbol
30. Uncooked
32. Near to
33. Objective case of I

solution 56

B	E	Y		L	W	E	I		I	L	L
I	B	E	X		A	E	O	N		R	U	E
T	B	A	R		C	A	N	A	D	I	A	N
		S	A	B	E	R		N	I	S	U	S
P	L	A	Y	E	R		P	E	P			
U	E	Y		T	A	W	S		P	S	S	T
S	T	E	P		T	E	A		Y	U	L	E
H	O	R	A		E	E	L	S		R	U	N
		L	S	D		M	I	F	F	E	D
I	B	S	E	N		E	B	B	E	D	
F	A	L	S	E	T	T	O		E	U	R	O
F	L	U		L	I	N	O		S	C	A	R
Y	E	R		L	E	A	K		K	G	B

ACROSS
1. Turkish governor
4. Monetary unit of Angola
8. Sick
11. Mountain goat
13. Great age
14. Regret
15. Type of automatic gear selector (1-3)
16. Inhabitant of Canada
18. Cavalry sword
20. Effort
21. Actor
23. Energy
24. U-turn (Colloq)
25. Leather whip
27. Surreptitious, attention getting sound
31. Pace
33. An infusion
34. Christmas
35. Israeli round dance
36. Long fish
38. Flee
39. Hallucinogenic drug
41. Ticked
43. Norwegian dramatist
46. Waned
47. Forced high notes
49. Wallaroo
52. Influenza
53. Floor covering
54. Old injury mark
55. Your (Colloq)
56. Lose water
57. Russian secret police

DOWN
1. Piece
2. Wane
3. Sycophant
4. Torn
5. Erode
6. An age
7. Vapid
8. Eye part
9. Hawaiian feast
10. Telescope part
12. Photograph of bones (1-3)
17. Foolish
19. Wager
21. Jostle
22. Mother of Apollo
23. Psalter
26. Tiny
28. Scoter
29. Swing around
30. Nurse
32. Fades
37. Kinsman
40. Fishhook line
42. Professional charges
43. Full of unresolved questions
44. Wool package
45. Elide
46. Sicilian volcano
48. Bind
50. Tatter
51. Sphere

solution 57

D	O	M	■	C	Y	M	E	B	A	A
A	H	O	Y	■	A	E	O	N	■	L	U	G
N	O	V	A	■	M	A	T	A	H	A	R	I
■	■	E	R	N	E	S	■	C	U	B	A	N
D	U	M	D	U	M	■	I	T	S	■
O	N	E	■	T	B	A	R	■	S	P	A	T
S	I	N	E	■	E	R	R	■	Y	O	G	I
E	T	T	E	■	R	E	I	N	■	S	U	E
■	■	R	O	T	■	T	E	E	T	E	R
S	T	A	I	N	■	J	A	D	E	D	■
L	O	V	E	S	E	A	T	■	L	A	S	E
E	G	O	■	E	A	V	E	■	S	T	O	L
W	A	N	■	T	R	A	D	■	E	N	D

ACROSS
1. Benedictine monk's title
4. Type of inflorescence
8. Bleat
11. Nautical call
13. Great age
14. Haul
15. Exploding star
16. Beautiful, seductive spy (4.4)
18. Sea eagles
20. Havana resident
21. Hollow-nosed bullet
23. Sexless things
24. Monad
25. Type of automatic gear selector (1-3)
27. Gaiter
31. Trigonometric function
33. Go wrong
34. Practitioner of yoga
35. Suffix, diminutive
36. Riding strap
38. Take to court
39. Decay
41. Sway
43. Blemish
46. Wearied
47. Chair for two persons
49. Cut with laser
52. The self
53. Roof overhang
54. Short take-off and landing aircraft
55. Ashen
56. Type of jazz
57. Finish

DOWN
1. Level of karate proficiency
2. Exclamation of surprise
3. Motion
4. Soft cheese
5. Shouts of agreement
6. Witty remark
7. Make law
8. Reveal secret
9. Subtle emanation
10. Against
12. Length measure
17. Lewd woman
19. Hard-shelled fruit
21. Measure of medicine
22. Military detachment
23. Vexed
26. Land measure
28. Follow in time
29. Fever
30. Row
32. Weird
37. - Kelly
40. Beginning
42. Long fish
43. Swing to the side
44. Roman garment
45. Shakespeare's river
46. Main island of Indonesia
48. Otic organ
50. Male offspring
51. Antiquity

solution 58

B	I	N		B	A	R	D		B	A	R
A	L	I	T		O	L	I	O		O	N	O
D	E	N	E		G	A	B	F	E	S	T	S
		E	A	S	E	R		F	I	N	I	S
A	F	F	R	A	Y		L	S	D			
L	E	O		O	S	L	O		E	R	A	S
T	E	L	E		H	E	R		R	I	L	E
O	L	D	S		O	D	D	S		G	O	A
			B	U	T		M	O	T	H	E	R
A	P	I	A	N		A	A	L	S	T		
T	E	R	T	I	A	R	Y		A	F	A	R
O	R	E		T	R	I	O		R	U	B	E
M	E	S		Y	E	A	R		L	Y	E	

ACROSS
1. Garbage can
4. Poet
8. Metal rod
11. Got down from mount
13. Potpourri
14. Yoko -
15. Sand dune
16. Conferences
18. Soother
20. The end
21. Brawl
23. Hallucinogenic drug
24. Zodiac sign
25. Capital of Norway
27. Periods of history
31. Prefix, distant
33. That woman
34. Anger
35. One's parents (Colloq)
36. Chances
38. Tibetan gazelle
39. However
41. A parent
43. Of bees
46. City in central Belgium
47. Third
49. Distant
52. Crude mineral
53. Threesome
54. Hick
55. My, French (Plural)
56. Long period of time
57. Soap ingredient

DOWN
1. Evil
2. Island (France)
3. Nine times as much
4. Golfing stroke resulting in one over par (5,4)
5. Having wings
6. Chest bone
7. Takes off (clothes)
8. Boatswain
9. Against
10. Antarctic explorer
12. Rip
17. Downy duck
19. Cracker biscuit
21. Singer
22. Sense
23. Chief municipal officer
26. Captained
28. Having a just claim
29. Agave
30. Scorch
32. Convocation of witches
37. The sun
40. Oneness
42. Russian emperor
43. Small particle
44. Father
45. Angers
46. Opera solo
48. Land measure
50. To endure
51. Female ruff

solution 59

P	O	T		C	A	P	E		O	R	B
E	I	R	E		O	R	E	S		P	U	L
P	L	A	Y		S	A	N	T	I	A	G	O
			C	R	U	M	B		E	C	L	A	T
E	S	T	A	T	E		P	R	O		
U	N	I		E	T	O	N		N	A	P	A
R	O	L	E		I	V	E		S	C	A	B
O	B	E	Y		C	A	U	L		C	R	U
			I	D	S		M	I	N	U	E	T
A	T	O	N	E		Q	A	T	A	R		
Z	I	G	G	U	R	A	T		V	A	I	N
O	L	E		C	E	D	I		E	T	N	A
V	E	E		E	P	I	C		E	K	E

ACROSS
1. Cooking implement
4. Cloak
8. Sphere
11. Ireland
13. Crude minerals
14. Monetary unit of Afghanistan
15. Stage show
16. Capital of Chile
18. Bread particle
20. Applause
21. Worldly goods
23. In favour of
24. Prefix, one
25. English college
27. Soft lambskin leather
31. Part played
33. I have
34. Strike breaker
35. Heed
36. Hood-like membrane
38. French vineyard
39. Egos
41. French dance
43. Make amends
46. Emirate on the Persian Gulf
47. Sumerian temple tower
49. Conceited
52. Bullfight call
53. Basic monetary unit of Ghana
54. Sicilian volcano
55. Victory sign
56. Heroic
57. Supplement existence

DOWN
1. Energy
2. Lubricant
3. Ductile
4. Makeup
5. Semite
6. Female swan
7. Chemical compound
8. Iridescent gem
9. Wrinkle
10. Ink stain
12. Jaguarundi
17. Images
19. Small truck
21. Wallaroo
22. Scorning person
23. Pertaining to air
26. Eggs
28. Free from error
29. Shave
30. Adjoin
32. Watching
37. Ignited
40. Tennis score
42. Wheel hub
43. Northern arm of the Black Sea
44. Roofing slate
45. Double curve
46. Muslim judge
48. Corded fabric
50. Writing fluid
51. Not

solution 60

I	D	E			C	H	A	R		H	E	L
C	O	M	E		L	U	R	E		O	D	A
Y	E	A	R		O	N	C	O	L	O	G	Y
		N	I	D	U	S		P	O	K	E	S
L	E	A	N	E	D		S	T	Y			
A	C	T		B	L	U	E		A	Z	A	N
P	R	E	P		I	S	M		L	O	R	E
P	U	S	H		K	E	A	S		O	C	A
			A	L	E		N	A	U	G	H	T
G	A	S	S	Y		S	T	O	P	E		
L	I	T	E	R	A	T	I		O	N	E	R
O	D	E		E	X	E	C		N	I	G	H
M	E	M		S	E	T	S		C	O	O	

ACROSS
1. Carp-like fish
4. Scorch
8. Norse goddess
11. Arrive
13. Tempt
14. Room within a harem
15. Long period of time
16. The treatment of cancer
18. Nest
20. Jabs
21. Tilted
23. Pig enclosure
24. Play division
25. Sky colour
27. Islamic call to prayer
31. Prepare patient for operation
33. Doctrine
34. Tradition
35. Jostle
36. New Zealand parrots
38. Wood sorrel
39. Beer
41. Zero
43. Effervescent
46. Mine excavation
47. Clerisy
49. Unique thing
52. Poem
53. Executive Officer
54. Near
55. 13th letter of the Hebrew alphabet
56. Hardens
57. Dove's call

DOWN
1. Gelid
2. Female deer
3. Issues
4. Nebulose
5. Vandals
6. Part of a circle
7. Re-choose
8. Crook
9. Brink
10. Puts down
12. Ireland
17. Faithful
19. Debutante
21. Scandinavian
22. Colour of unbleached linen
23. Semasiology
26. Avail of
28. Caused by animals
29. Curved entrance
30. Tidy
32. Stage
37. Cracker biscuit
40. Harp-like instruments
42. On top of
43. Glimpse
44. Assistant
45. Stalk
46. Printer's mark, keep
48. Chop
50. The self
51. 17th letter of the Greek alphabet

solution 61

J	A	B		D	H	A	L		R	P	M
I	C	O	N		Y	U	L	E		I	O	U
G	E	N	U		S	L	E	E	P	E	R	S
		A	K	E	L	A		R	A	L	E	S
E	F	F	E	T	E		A	Y	E			
E	L	I		A	C	E	R		A	R	C	H
L	A	D	E		T	A	G		N	I	L	E
S	K	E	W		I	R	E	D		N	U	N
		E	T	C		N	U	D	G	E	S	
A	C	C	R	A		S	T	E	A	D		
H	E	L	S	I	N	K	I		T	O	R	O
O	R	E		G	A	I	T		E	V	E	N
Y	E	W		A	N	T	E			E	V	E

ACROSS
1. Poke
4. Indian pulses
8. Rotational speed
11. Image
13. Christmas
14. Acknowledgement of debt
15. Knee
16. Railway ties
18. Cub leader
20. Breathes rattlingly
21. Exhausted
23. Affirmative vote
24. Biblical high priest
25. The maple
27. Curved entrance
31. Burden
33. Label
34. African river
35. Oblique
36. Angered
38. Cloistered woman
39. Etcetera
41. Pokes with elbow
43. Capital of Ghana
46. Place
47. Capital of Finland
49. Bull
52. Crude mineral
53. Walk
54. Level
55. Evergreen tree
56. Poker stake
57. First woman

DOWN
1. Lively dance
2. Top card
3. Authentic
4. One who has a reading ability impairment
5. Hawaiian dance
6. Beer
7. Wary
8. Monetary unit of Cambodia
9. Skin opening
10. Rumple
12. Use atomic bom on (Colloq)
17. Song of praise
19. Greek letter
21. Long fish
22. Antiaircraft fire
23. Silver sulfide
26. Otic organ
28. Small domestic dove
29. A hint
30. Female birds
32. Pitchers
37. Owing
40. Coniferous evergreen forest
42. An appointment
43. Nautical call
44. Wax
45. Skein of thread
46. Short parody
48. Grandmother
50. Speed up motor
51. Monad

solution 62

A	Y	E	■	T	O	P	S	■	A	G	O
L	O	A	D	■	O	D	I	N	■	P	A	W
L	U	S	H	■	L	E	G	A	T	I	O	N
■	■	T	A	T	E	R	■	C	O	A	L	S
H	O	W	L	E	R	■	E	K	E	■	■	■
A	H	A	■	A	A	H	S	■	A	V	E	R
F	I	R	E	■	B	I	P	■	S	I	V	A
T	O	D	O	■	L	E	E	K	■	T	I	T
■	■	■	S	H	E	■	R	E	G	A	L	E
S	A	D	I	E	■	B	A	G	E	L	■	■
C	H	I	N	A	M	A	N	■	N	I	G	H
A	O	K	■	D	I	S	C	■	S	T	O	A
B	Y	E	■	Y	A	T	E	■	Y	A	M	■

ACROSS
1. Affirmative vote
4. Spinning toys
8. In the past
11. A burden
13. Norse god
14. Dog's foot
15. Luxuriant
16. Envoy's office
18. Potato (Colloq)
20. Embers
21. Bawler
23. Supplement existence
24. Exclamation of surprise
25. Exclamations of surprise
27. Vow
31. Flame
33. Beep horn
34. Hindu god of destruction
35. Bustle or fuss (Colloq) (2-2)
36. Welsh emblem
38. Small bird
39. That woman
41. Entertain
43. Cleaning lady
46. Doughnut-shaped roll
47. A seric
49. Near
52. Very good (1-2)
53. Circular plate
54. Portico
55. Farewell
56. W.A. eucalypt
57. Sweet potato

DOWN
1. Everything
2. Yourself
3. Towards the orient
4. Able to be put up with
5. River in central Europe
6. Hog
7. Light meal
8. Capital of Western Samoa
9. Jail
10. 3 Admits
12. Indian pulses
17. New Guinea currency units
19. An infusion
21. Handle of a knife
22. U.S. State
23. Western Australian coastal town
26. Hasten
28. Vigor
29. Sinister
30. Assess
32. Red dye
37. Beer barrel
40. Intoxicating
42. Clan
43. Strike breaker
44. Nautical call
45. Levee
46. Strong woody fiber
48. Actress, - Farrow
50. Tibetan gazelle
51. Overact

solution 63

H	U	G		S	K	I	D		E	M	S
A	N	E	W	H	A	R	E		M	I	A
M	I	T	E	E	L	E	C	T	I	N	G
		A	D	D	L	E		A	E	R	I	E
L	O	W	S	E	T		I	F	S		
O	V	A		E	E	L	S		L	A	O	S
S	A	Y	S		R	I	O		A	C	R	E
E	L	S	E		E	D	G	E		T	A	R
			W	E	D		E	T	O	I	L	E
A	N	G	E	L		A	N	C	O	N		
C	A	U	D	I	L	L	O		P	I	T	H
H	I	S		T	U	T	U		S	U	R	A
E	F	T		E	G	O	S		M	I	D	

ACROSS
1. Embrace
4. Slide
8. Printer's measures
11. Once again
13. Fleet rodent
14. Actress, - Farrow
15. Small spider
16. Choosing
18. Muddle
20. Eagle's nest
21. Descriptive of a house built on a concrete slab
23. Possibilities
24. Eggs
25. Long fish
27. South-east Asian nation
31. States
33. - de Janeiro
34. Land measure
35. Otherwise
36. Brink
38. Road surfacing
39. Marry
41. Star (Heraldry)
43. Seraph
46. The elbow
47. Military dictator
49. Gist
52. Belonging to him
53. Ballet skirt
54. Chapter of the Koran
55. Newt
56. Personalities
57. Among

DOWN
1. Overact
2. Prefix, one
3. Escapes
4. Protected
5. Cabbagelike plant
6. Anger
7. Decaffeinated
8. Islamic chieftain
9. Short dress
10. Wise
12. Marries
17. Unit of magnetic induction
19. Scottish river
21. Be defeated
22. Egg-shaped
23. Having the same origin
26. Bottle top
28. Radioactive metallic element
29. Spoken
30. Withered
32. Stitched
37. Etcetera
40. The cream
42. Expression used when accident happens
43. Pain
44. Naive person
45. Sudden blow
46. Singer
48. Haul
50. Prefix, three
51. Possessed

solution 64

Y	A	K		L	W	E	I		S	B	S
E	M	I	T		E	A	R	L		N	A	E
N	U	D	E		A	L	G	I	C	I	D	E
		G	N	A	R	L		U	R	G	E	R
N	E	L	S	O	N		A	M	U			
A	D	O		K	I	N	G		D	A	N	S
S	A	V	E		N	E	O		E	S	A	U
A	M	E	N		G	E	N	E		S	I	R
		A	S	S		I	T	S	E	L	F	
E	D	U	C	E		P	S	A	L	M		
P	O	R	T	R	A	I	T		A	B	L	E
I	D	A		I	N	T	I		G	L	E	E
C	O	L		F	I	S	C		Y	I	N	

ACROSS
1. Tibetan ox
4. Monetary unit of Angola
8. Ethnic telecaster
11. Send out
13. Nobleman
14. Not
15. Naked
16. Preparation for killing algae
18. Knot
20. Tout
21. Trafalgar hero
23. Atomic mass unit
24. Fuss
25. Monarch
27. Levels of karate proficiency
31. Rescue
33. Prefix, new
34. Son of Isaac and Rebekah
35. Prayer ending
36. Hereditary factor
38. Knight's title
39. Donkey
41. Emphatic form of it
43. Draw forth
46. Hymn
47. Likeness of a person
49. Capable
52. Highest mountain in Crete
53. Monetary unit of Peru
54. Merriment
55. Mountain pass
56. Exchequer
57. - and Yang

DOWN
1. Japanese currency
2. Atomic mass unit
3. Glove made of kid leather
4. One's acquired knowledge
5. Building side
6. Work unit
7. Hipbone
8. Drag logs
9. Past tense of bid
10. Prophet
12. Decades
17. Unrefined
19. Very good (1-2)
21. U.S. space agency
22. Dutch cheese
23. Combative
26. Born
28. Gathering
29. Metal spike
30. Breakers
32. Make law
37. Greek letter
40. Letter cross-line
42. Metal dross
43. Heroic
44. Extinct bird
45. European mountain range
46. Mines
48. Black bird
50. Garland
51. Even (poet.)

solution 65

R	O	O		A	L	A	S		E	R	G
E	D	E	N		D	A	R	K		P	I	E
P	A	N	E		H	U	M	A	N	I	S	M
		O	A	R	E	D		L	A	C	K	S
F	A	L	T	E	R		A	D	Z			
A	D	O		T	E	A	L		I	M	A	M
D	I	G	S		N	I	L		S	A	G	E
S	T	Y	E		C	R	A	B		N	U	N
		P	O	E		R	A	I	D	E	D	
S	E	P	I	K		A	O	R	T	A		
K	R	A	K	A	T	A	U		E	M	I	T
Y	I	N		P	O	R	N		M	U	C	H
E	N	S		I	R	E	D		S	E	E	

ACROSS
1. Kangaroo
4. Woe is me
8. Work unit
11. Paradise
13. Murky
14. Pastry item
15. Glass panel
16. Devotion to the humanities
18. Rowed
20. Doesn't have
21. Hesitate
23. Axlike tool
24. Fuss
25. Freshwater duck
27. Officiating priest of a mosque
31. Excavates
33. Zero
34. Wise
35. Eye inflammation
36. Crustacean
38. Cloistered woman
39. "The Raven" author
41. Secretly attacked
43. Papua and New Guinea river
46. Major artery
47. Indonesian volcano
49. Send out
52. - and Yang
53. Pornography (Colloq)
54. Greatly
55. Abstract being
56. Angered
57. Witness

DOWN
1. Corded fabric
2. Room within a harem
3. Science of winemaking
4. Allegiance
5. Praise
6. Limb
7. Scandinavian poet
8. Heroic
9. Endanger
10. Jewels
12. Tidy
17. Hitler's followers
19. Soak flax
21. Crazes
22. Entrance
23. Versatile
26. Atmosphere
28. A superior court writ
29. Fever
30. Repair
32. Papua and New Guinea river
37. Metal rod
40. Giraffe-like animal
42. A particular
43. Inner Hebrides island
44. Ireland
45. Kitchen utensils
46. River in central Switzerland
48. Rocky peak
50. Freeze
51. Definite article

solution 66

E	R	S			E	K	E	S		S	H	E
O	A	K	S		X	E	R	O		W	A	R
N	Y	E	T		N	A	G	A	S	A	K	I
		E	U	R	U	S		P	E	K	E	S
C	A	T	N	A	P		P	S	I			
A	L	E		P	T	A	H		N	A	I	F
R	A	R	E		I	D	O		E	L	S	E
E	R	S	T		A	S	T	I		L	I	E
			H	E	L		O	L	D	E	S	T
O	N	I	O	N		S	P	L	A	Y		
C	O	I	S	T	R	E	L		S	C	U	D
T	O	W		I	O	T	A		H	A	T	E
A	N	I		A	W	A	Y		T	E	E	

ACROSS
1. Bitter vetch
4. Supplements
8. That woman
11. Large trees
13. Prefix, dry
14. Battle
15. Russian no
16. Seaport on W Kyushu
18. The east wind
20. Small dogs
21. Short, light sleep
23. Pressure symbol
24. Beer
25. Egyptian deity
27. Naive person
31. Uncommon
33. Revised form of Esperanto
34. Otherwise
35. Former
36. Italian wine province
38. Falsehood
39. Norse goddess
41. Most senior
43. Bulb vegetable
46. Spread
47. Scoundrel
49. Driving shower
52. Haul
53. Jot
54. Detest
55. Black bird
56. Absent
57. Golf peg

DOWN
1. An age
2. Sunbeam
3. Mosquitoes (Colloq)
4. Outside marriage
5. New Zealand parrots
6. Work unit
7. Lathers
8. Sealed with a kiss
9. Codlike fish
10. Greek goddess of strife
12. Daze
17. Fishing net
19. Knock with knuckles
21. Attention
22. Having wings
23. Screenplay
26. Commercials
28. Cat of unknown parentage
29. Egyptian goddess of fertility
30. Length measures
32. Spirit
37. Sick
40. Abstract beings
42. Sprint
43. Prefix, eight
44. Midday
45. Hawaiian honeycreeper
46. Bristle
48. Tier
50. Small truck
51. Scottish river

solution 67

L	E	N		N	A	I	F		N	E	B
E	B	O	N		O	L	L	A		Y	A	O
O	B	I	E		M	E	E	K	N	E	S	S
		S	A	D	I	E		E	A	T	E	N
T	R	E	P	A	N		A	S	H			
H	E	T		N	A	R	C		U	M	B	O
U	N	T	O		L	E	U		M	A	I	N
G	O	E	R		L	E	T	O		J	E	T
	A	N	Y		E	N	T	E	R	O		
S	U	L	L	A		K	N	O	B	S		
P	R	I	S	T	I	N	E		A	T	O	M
A	G	E		A	C	E	S		R	I	P	E
Y	E	N		L	E	E	S		C	E	T	

ACROSS
1. Pet form of Leonard
4. Naive person
8. Beak
11. Black
13. Earthen pot
14. Legendary emperor of China
15. Off-Broadway theater award
16. Humility
18. Cleaning lady
20. Consumed
21. Surgical saw
23. Fire remains
24. - up, excited
25. Narcotics agent
27. Boss on a shield
31. To
33. Monetary unit of Romania
34. Chief
35. Apparently successful project
36. Mother of Apollo
38. Black
39. Some
41. Prefix, intestine
43. Roman general
46. Door handles
47. Having original purity
49. Small particle
52. Mature
53. Beats by tennis service
54. Mature
55. Japanese currency
56. Dregs
57. Prefix, whale

DOWN
1. Zodiac sign
2. Wane
3. Boned cutlet
4. In name only
5. To the sheltered side
6. Island (France)
7. Feigns
8. Russian no
9. Relax
10. Boatswain
12. Lowest high tide
17. Book of the Bible
19. Level of karate proficiency
21. Brutal gangster
22. U.S. divorce city
23. Acuity
26. Female ruff
28. Imposing
29. Coffin stand
30. Upon
32. Verbal exams
37. Yoko -
40. Of birth
42. Type of automatic gear selector (1-3)
43. Desex female dog
44. Incite
45. Charge over property
46. Leg joint
48. Freeze
50. Open
51. Greeted

solution 68

R	A	Y		M	O	T	T		O	W	L
O	P	A	L		A	D	A	R		B	E	E
Y	E	T	I		L	E	G	A	C	I	E	S
		A	N	E	A	R		P	E	E	K	S
E	G	G	N	O	G		L	S	D			
R	A	H		N	U	D	E		A	G	R	A
I	M	A	M		E	R	G		R	U	I	N
N	E	N	E		N	Y	E	T		E	F	T
			A	H	A		N	A	U	S	E	A
S	H	O	N	E		E	D	E	N	S		
M	A	N	T	I	L	L	A		C	I	S	T
U	L	T		S	E	A	R		O	N	E	R
G	E	O		T	I	N	Y		G	A	Y	

ACROSS
1. Sunbeam
4. Clump of trees
8. Nocturnal bird
11. Iridescent gem
13. 6th month of the Jewish calendar
14. Hive insect
15. Abominable snowman
16. Bequests
18. Anigh
20. Takes a quick look at
21. Milk and egg drink
23. Hallucinogenic drug
24. Cheer
25. Naked
27. Taj Mahal site
31. Officiating priest of a mosque
33. Work unit
34. Wreck
35. Hawaiian goose
36. Russian no
38. Newt
39. Exclamation of surprise
41. Sickness of stomach
43. Glowed
46. Paradises
47. Lace scarf
49. Prehistoric sepulchral tomb
52. Last month
53. Scorch
54. Unique thing
55. Prefix, the earth
56. Wee
57. Merry

DOWN
1. - Rene. Mo
2. Primate
3. Turkish sword
4. Spanish dance
5. River in central Europe
6. Label
7. Snares
8. Off-Broadway theater award
9. Seven days
10. Minus
12. Waterfall
17. Timber tree
19. An age
21. Ireland
22. Brave
23. Pertaining to a legend
26. Arid
28. Surmising
29. Prevalent
30. Rectangular pier
32. Intended
37. - kwon do (Korean martial art)
40. Robbery
42. Remarkable
43. Complacent
44. Robust
45. Upon
46. Dash
48. Garland
50. Large body of water
51. Attempt

solution 69

D	O	T		D	O	T	E		T	A	R
A	B	E	D		E	N	O	W		O	D	A
B	I	R	O		M	E	T	E	O	R	I	C
		A	L	T	A	R		R	U	T	T	Y
S	U	T	L	E	R		E	S	T			
O	N	O		E	C	R	U		R	E	A	L
A	I	M	S		A	I	R		E	N	V	Y
P	T	A	H		T	B	A	R		T	O	R
			I	C	E		S	A	L	I	N	E
	S	H	I	V	A		E	I	D	E	R	
M	E	L	A	N	O	M	A		E	E	L	S
I	R	K		E	R	I	N		S	T	A	B
T	E	A		S	E	T	S		Y	E	S	

ACROSS
1. Speck
4. Be foolishly fond of
8. Road surfacing
11. In bed
13. Enough
14. Room within a harem
15. Pen
16. Pertaining to meteors
18. Sacrificial bench
20. Full of ruts
21. Victualer
23. Superlative suffix
24. Yoko -
25. Colour of unbleached linen
27. Genuine
31. Intentions
33. Atmosphere
34. Jealousy
35. Egyptian deity
36. Type of automatic gear selector (1-3)
38. Rocky peak
39. Freeze
41. Salt solution
43. The Hindu Destroyer
46. Downy duck
47. Skin tumor
49. Long fish
52. Vex
53. Ireland
54. Pierce with knife
55. An infusion
56. Hardens
57. Affirmative response

DOWN
1. Skilled
2. Japanese sash
3. Tumor
4. Mark out boundaries of
5. Unique thing
6. Young child
7. Pitchers
8. Misdeed
9. Entrance
10. Risque
12. Girl's plaything
17. Bizarre
19. Golf peg
21. Bath requisite
22. Military detachment
23. People of European/Asian derivation
26. Chest bone
28. Completeness
29. Shakespeare's river
30. Harp-like instrument
32. The Hindu Destroyer
37. Radiation unit
40. Walking sticks
42. Dregs
43. Struck
44. In this place
45. Every
46. Send out
48. Crude mineral
50. New Guinea seaport
51. Ethnic telecaster

solution 70

T	I	N		U	T	A	H		G	U	N
O	D	E	S		N	I	C	E		E	R	E
W	A	S	H		F	E	E	L	I	N	G	S
		T	U	M	I	D		O	N	S	E	T
W	A	L	N	U	T		A	T	E			
O	B	I		G	N	A	W		P	L	A	N
R	E	N	D		E	R	A		T	O	F	U
E	D	G	E		S	E	R	B		V	A	N
			M	E	S		E	I	D	E	R	S
O	N	I	O	N		S	N	O	E	K		
L	A	M	B	A	S	T	E		S	N	O	B
L	O	P		C	U	E	S		K	O	L	O
A	S	S		T	E	N	S		T	E	A	

ACROSS
1. Metal can
4. American state
8. Firearm
11. Poems
13. Pleasing
14. Before
15. Cleanse
16. Sentiments
18. Swollen
20. Beginning
21. Nut variety
23. Dined
24. Japanese sash
25. Chew on a bone
27. Scheme
31. Tear
33. An age
34. Beancurd
35. Brink
36. Yugoslavian
38. Forefront
39. My, French (Plural)
41. Downy ducks
43. Bulb vegetable
46. Barracouta
47. Beat severely
49. Scorning person
52. Cut off
53. Prompts
54. Serbian folk dance
55. Donkey
56. Decades
57. An infusion

DOWN
1. Haul
2. Highest mountain in Crete
3. Very young bird
4. Inaptitude
5. Bound
6. Top card
7. Spartan serf
8. Clan
9. Incite
10. Nidus
12. Avoid
17. Inappropriate
19. Drinking vessel
21. Eroded
22. In bed
23. Consciousness
26. Land measure
28. Ribbon emblematic of love
29. Distant
30. Cloistered women
32. Disband troops
37. Prefix, life
40. Make law
42. Writing table
43. Earthen pot
44. Temple
45. Little devils
46. Submachine gun
48. Take to court
50. Bullfight call
51. Large snake

solution 71

A	L	P		A	F	A	R		G	E	L
X	E	R	O		N	E	R	O		O	D	A
E	D	A	M		C	A	C	O	L	O	G	Y
		C	A	R	E	T		M	O	D	E	S
E	X	T	R	A	S		P	S	I			
T	R	I		P	T	A	H		N	I	B	S
T	A	C	K		O	H	O		S	O	O	T
E	Y	E	R		R	A	N	D		D	O	E
		I	D	S		E	O	N	I	S	M	
S	C	A	L	E		E	T	H	O	S		
K	O	H	L	R	A	B	I		V	I	C	E
I	D	O		B	L	O	C		A	N	O	N
D	A	Y		Y	E	N	S		G	O	D	

ACROSS
1. Peak
4. Distant
8. Congeal
11. Prefix, dry
13. Fiddling Roman emperor
14. Room within a harem
15. Dutch cheese
16. Defective pronunciation
18. Mark of omission
20. Styles
21. Cricket sundries
23. Pressure symbol
24. Prefix, three
25. Egyptian deity
27. Person in authority
31. Small nail
33. Exclamation of surprise
34. Coal dust
35. Looker
36. South African currency
38. Female deer
39. Egos
41. Transvestism
43. Climb
46. Spirit
47. Cultivated cabbage
49. An evil
52. Revised form of Esperanto
53. Political combine
54. Soon
55. Time of sunshine
56. Desires
57. Deity

DOWN
1. Chop
2. Captained
3. Custom
4. Forebears
5. Exploit
6. Part of a circle
7. House parts
8. Benevolent
9. Brink
10. Puts down
12. - Khayyam
17. Hips
19. Knock with knuckles
21. Suffix, diminutive
22. Photograph of bones (1-3)
23. Study of speech sounds
26. Exclamation of surprise
28. Treating with iodine
29. Jeers
30. Stalk
32. Small crustaceans eaten by whales
37. Scale note
40. Horse race
42. Exploding star
43. Slide
44. Musical ending
45. Nautical call
46. Black
48. Beer
50. Dove's call
51. Finish

solution 72

ACROSS
1. Drinking vessel
4. Songbird
8. Open
11. Once again
13. Prefix, sun
14. Humour
15. Pen
16. Person's individual speech pattern
18. Packs fully
20. Murder by suffocation
21. Purgative injections
23. Monetary unit of Japan
24. Colorful form of the common carp
25. Rube
27. Beaten by tennis service
31. Roof overhang
33. - Guevara
34. Hindu music
35. Outbuilding
36. Assistant
38. Singer, - "King" Cole
39. Conger
41. Battle fleet
43. Slope
46. Grass trimming tool
47. Ate
49. Stead
52. Talent
53. Girl's plaything
54. Rip
55. Change colour of
56. Relax
57. Underwater craft

DOWN
1. Taxi
2. Prefix, one
3. See
4. Capricious
5. Clarets
6. Biblical high priest
7. Zeus changed her to stone
8. One who is indebted
9. Select
10. Suffix, diminutive
12. Annelid
17. Of the moon
19. Exclamation of surprise
21. Supplements
22. Ark builder
23. Hasty flight
26. Greek letter
28. Pet birds
29. Minor oath
30. Information
32. Paradises
37. Work unit
40. Musical study piece
42. Thaw
43. Great quantity
44. Lorikeet
45. Poker stake
46. Long fish
48. New Zealand bird
50. French, water
51. An urban area

solution 73

B	I	B		E	G	G	S		P	I	T
O	D	E	R		X	R	A	Y		U	T	E
X	E	N	O		P	E	T	R	O	L	I	C
		J	O	K	E	Y		I	R	I	S	H
R	E	A	M	E	D		L	A	C			
A	I	M		N	I	P	A		A	T	O	M
G	R	I	D		E	L	K		S	A	G	E
G	E	N	U		N	Y	E	T		R	E	E
		C	E	T		P	O	O	L	E	D	
S	P	L	A	Y		A	O	R	T	A		
T	A	I	L	R	A	C	E		I	T	E	M
A	T	E		I	S	N	T		C	A	R	E
B	E	D		E	K	E	S		N	A	M	

ACROSS
1. Infant's protective garment
4. Ova
8. Mine
11. River in central Europe
13. Photograph of bones (1-3)
14. Small truck
15. Prefix, foreign
16. Produced from petroleum
18. Given to joking
20. Erse
21. Bored out
23. Resinous deposit
24. Intention
25. East Indies palm
27. Small particle
31. Network
33. Moose
34. Wise
35. Knee
36. Russian no
38. Female ruff
39. Prefix, whale
41. Combined resources
43. Spread
46. Major artery
47. Channel leading away
49. A particular
52. Dined
53. Is not
54. Attention
55. Cot
56. Supplements
57. Vietnam

DOWN
1. Crate
2. Carp-like fish
3. One of the tribes of Israel
4. Means to an end
5. Hoar
6. Gun (Slang)
7. Its capital is Damascus
8. Hungarian sheepdog
9. Inflammation (Suffix)
10. Technical college (Colloq)
12. Space
17. Killer whales
19. Knowledge
21. Sturdy wool fiber
22. Ireland
23. Wordsworth, Coleridge, and Southey (4,5)
26. 3 Thickness
28. Muslin
29. Double curve
30. Reward
32. Of a Duke
37. Rocky peak
40. Eagle's nest
42. Auricular
43. Pierce with knife
44. Meat paste
45. Prevaricated
46. Adolescent pimples
48. Question
50. An age
51. 13th letter of the Hebrew alphabet

solution 74

B	O	T			A	W	A	Y		P	E	D
U	P	O	N		P	A	N	E		A	L	E
N	E	R	O		O	L	Y	M	P	I	A	N
		E	P	A	C	T		E	A	R	N	S
S	E	A	E	A	R		E	N	D			
A	D	D		H	Y	L	A		D	Y	A	D
S	N	O	W		P	A	R		Y	A	L	E
H	A	R	E		H	E	T	H		R	O	E
		I	S	A		H	I	N	D	E	R	
S	I	E	G	E		D	W	E	E	B		
C	A	T	H	E	D	R	A		A	I	D	E
A	G	O		P	I	E	R		T	R	I	O
B	O	N		S	P	E	D		D	E	N

ACROSS
1. Fly larva
4. Absent
8. Prefix, foot
11. On top of
13. Glass panel
14. Beer
15. Fiddling Roman emperor
16. Contender in the Olympic Games
18. Moon age at start of year
20. Works for
21. Abalone (3,3)
23. Finish
24. Sum
25. Tree frog
27. Group of two
31. Frozen precipitation
33. Normal
34. American university
35. Fleet rodent
36. 8th letter of the Hebrew alphabet
38. Fish eggs
39. Mount - , N.W. Qld. mining town
41. Hamper
43. Blockade
46. Nerd
47. Throne of a bishop
49. Assistant
52. In the past
53. Jetty
54. Threesome
55. French, good
56. Raced
57. Lair

DOWN
1. Bread roll
2. Open
3. Bullfighter
4. Religious writings
5. - Disney
6. Some
7. Arab country
8. Duo
9. Dash
10. Lairs
12. No (Colloq)
17. Rice field
19. Exclamation of surprise
21. Broad ribbon
22. Dame - Everage, Humphries' character
23. Toward the earth
26. New Guinea seaport
28. Convict
29. Agave
30. Antlered beast
32. Find weight of
37. Hasten
40. Oozes
42. Tidy
43. Strike breaker
44. The villain in Othello
45. English college
46. Endure
48. Briefly immerse in water
50. Expire
51. An age

solution 75

C	R	U		N	I	B	S		U	L	T
A	U	N	T		A	D	E	N		R	I	O
W	E	A	R		I	L	L	U	M	I	N	E
		R	I	N	S	E		B	A	C	K	S
D	O	G	M	A	S		A	S	P			
E	A	U		E	A	S	E		L	U	K	E
C	H	E	F		N	O	R		E	T	N	A
K	U	D	U		C	H	O	P		E	O	S
			S	H	E		D	A	I	N	T	Y
B	A	S	S	O		C	Y	S	T	S		
E	M	P	Y	R	E	A	N		I	I	W	I
A	M	U		D	A	T	E		S	L	A	V
T	O	D		E	R	O	S			S	T	Y

ACROSS
1. French vineyard
4. Person in authority
8. Last month
11. Female relative
13. Capital of Yemen
14. - de Janeiro
15. Erode
16. Illuminate
18. Wash out
20. Rears
21. Tenets
23. Egyptian serpent
24. French, water
25. Relax
27. One of the Disciples
31. Head cook
33. And not
34. Sicilian volcano
35. African antelope
36. Hew
38. Greek goddess of the dawn
39. That woman
41. Of delicate beauty
43. Bass singer
46. Wens
47. The heavens
49. Hawaiian honeycreeper
52. Atomic mass unit
53. An appointment
54. European race
55. Fox
56. Greek god of love
57. Pig enclosure

DOWN
1. Crow call
2. Regret
3. Undisputed
4. Birth
5. Lazy
6. Unit of loudness
7. Ignores
8. Of urine
9. Nexus
10. Pedal digits
12. Decorate (Xmas tree)
17. Tree
19. Not
21. Ship's floor
22. Island of Hawaii
23. Heavier-than-air craft
26. Scale note
28. Kitchen implements
29. Nautical mile
30. Simple
32. Hard to please
37. Dance step
40. Multitude
42. Inflammation (Suffix)
43. Vanquish
44. Ammunition (Colloq)
45. Potato (Colloq)
46. Roman censor
48. Otic organ
50. Buddhist temple
51. Climbing plant

solution 76

Z	E	I	N		P	R	O	D		Y	E	N
O	G	L	E		R	U	N	E		A	T	E
O	G	E	E		I	L	E	X		R	U	T
			D	O	L	E		T	U	N	I	S
R	U	E	F	U	L		C	E	P			
I	N	P	U	T		S	U	R		L	E	U
S	T	O	L		N	O	T		L	A	P	S
E	O	S		H	I	T		S	I	R	E	S
			M	A	B		W	I	L	D	E	R
N	A	V	E	L		A	I	R	Y			
E	L	I		L	O	P	S		P	O	R	K
A	L	L		E	R	I	E		A	L	O	E
R	Y	E		Y	E	A	R		D	E	W	Y

ACROSS
1. Maize protein
5. Jab
9. Japanese currency
12. Leer
13. Mysterious symbol
14. Dined
15. Double curve
16. Holly
17. Groove
18. Apportion
20. Capital of Tunisia
22. Full of regret
25. Brown-capped boletus mushroom
26. Contribution to discussion
27. Prefix, over
28. Monetary unit of Romania
31. Short take-off and landing aircraft
32. Negating word
33. Circuits
34. Greek goddess of the dawn
35. Strike
36. Fathers
37. Fairy queen
38. Lose one's way
39. Belly button
42. Well ventilated
43. Biblical high priest
44. Cuts off
46. Pig meat
50. Everything
51. A Great Lake
52. Agave
53. Cereal
54. Long period of time
55. Moist with dew

DOWN
1. Menagerie
2. Ovum
3. Island (France)
4. Necessary
5. Pelletize
6. Govern
7. Monad
8. The right side
9. Story
10. Sewing case
11. Devices for fishing
19. Not at home
21. Toward the top
22. Stand
23. To
24. Epic poetry
25. Sever
27. Drunkard
28. Fat
29. Fencing sword
30. Former Soviet Union
32. Pen point
33. Floating leaf
35. English astronomer
36. Knight's title
37. Objective case of I
38. More sensible
39. Close to
40. Friend
41. Evil
42. Capital of Western Samoa
45. Crude mineral
47. Bullfight call
48. Tier
49. Unlocking implement

solution 77

F	L	E	D		M	O	S	S		S	P	A
E	A	S	Y		A	P	I	A		P	A	P
Y	E	T	I		V	A	N	S		A	G	E
				N	A	I	L		H	A	R	E	S
H	A	G	G	I	S		H	A	M			
A	T	O	L	L		B	U	Y		A	I	D
T	O	R	Y		R	A	H		L	I	N	O
S	P	Y		G	I	T		B	A	N	T	U
		D	A	M		S	A	N	T	I	R	
S	H	E	O	L		A	U	N	T			
E	E	L		L	O	G	E		A	R	M	S
E	R	A		I	R	E	D		N	Y	E	T
M	E	N		C	E	D	E		A	E	R	Y

ACROSS
1. Ran from
5. Lichen
9. Mineral spring
12. Simple
13. Capital of Western Samoa
14. Nipple
15. Abominable snowman
16. Delivery vehicles
17. Mature
18. Metal spike
20. Fleet rodents
22. Scottish pudding
25. Overact
26. Coral island
27. Purchase
28. Assist
31. Member of the Conservative Party
32. Cheer
33. Floor covering
34. Secret agent
35. British, a fool
36. African tribe
37. Weir
38. Persian musical instrument
39. Abode of the dead
42. Female relative
43. Conger
44. Booth
46. 3 Weapons
50. An age
51. Angered
52. Russian no
53. Soldiers
54. Yield
55. Ethereal

DOWN
1. Doomed
2. New Guinea seaport
3. Superlative suffix
4. Deathly
5. Song thrush
6. Iridescent gem
7. Transgress
8. Walk nonchalantly
9. Mast
10. Book leaf
11. Primates
19. Sicken
21. Part of the verb "to be"
22. Headwear
23. At the apex
24. Bloody
25. Questioning exclamation
27. Flying mammal
28. Isn't
29. Monetary unit of Peru
30. Gloomy
32. Edge
33. Troublesome tropical plant grown for hedges and flowers
35. Characteristically French
36. Prohibit
37. Perform
38. Soft leather
39. Appear
40. In this place
41. Dash
42. Old
45. Crude mineral
47. Cereal
48. Sea (French)
49. Pig enclosure

solution 78

T	O	O	L		B	I	F	F		C	A	B
A	C	R	E		R	O	I	L		I	R	E
P	A	C	A		A	W	R	Y		T	E	D
			V	I	V	A		R	H	E	A	S
A	I	K	I	D	O		K	O	I			
S	W	A	N	S		C	I	D		G	Y	M
T	I	N	G		T	O	D		C	R	E	E
I	S	A		Y	A	P		S	H	A	L	T
			S	E	T		D	O	A	B	L	E
C	O	C	O	A		X	E	N	O			
U	G	H		N	A	M	E		T	A	B	S
E	L	I		E	D	A	M		I	L	I	A
D	E	N		D	O	S	S		C	E	N	T

ACROSS
1. Implement
5. Punch
9. Taxi
12. Land measure
13. Vex
14. Anger
15. Large almost tailless rodent
16. Askew
17. Spread out for drying
18. Exclamation of acclaim
20. Ostrich-like birds
22. Japanese form of self-defense
25. Colorful form of the common carp
26. Graceful birds
27. Spanish hero
28. Gymnasium
31. High, clear ringing sound
32. Fox
33. American Indian
34. Mount - , N.W. Qld. mining town
35. Yelp
36. Shall (Archaic)
37. Become firm
38. Capable of being done
39. Chocolate powder
42. Prefix, foreign
43. Expression of disgust
44. Title
46. Labels
50. Biblical high priest
51. Dutch cheese
52. Hip bones
53. Lair
54. Make temporary sleeping place (Colloq)
55. Monetary unit

DOWN
1. Faucet
2. Wood sorrel
3. Killer whale
4. Food scrap
5. Applause
6. U.S. State
7. An evergreen
8. Fishing rod
9. Quote
10. Region
11. Cots
19. Egos
21. Hello there
22. Italian wine province
23. Certainly
24. Japanese syllabic script
25. Young goat
27. Policeman
28. Clutch
29. Shout
30. Measure out
32. Make lace
33. Disordered
35. Lambed
36. Male offspring
37. Therefore
38. Considers
39. Prompted
40. Leer
41. Facial feature
42. Christmas
45. Fuss
47. Beer
48. Garbage can
49. Took a seat

solution 79

O	D	D	S	■	O	P	A	L	■	R	O	B
P	O	E	M	■	P	A	N	E	■	E	R	A
S	E	R	E	■	E	P	I	C	■	A	C	T
■	■	■	A	N	N	A	■	H	O	R	A	E
M	A	D	R	A	S	■	F	E	N	■	■	■
A	G	R	E	E	■	W	A	R	■	G	A	R
R	E	A	D	■	N	O	N	■	F	O	R	E
E	R	G	■	B	A	G	■	B	A	B	E	S
■	■	■	D	O	G	■	L	A	V	I	S	H
S	Y	N	O	D	■	I	A	G	O	■	■	■
K	E	A	■	I	S	N	T	■	R	E	E	D
E	A	R	■	L	O	C	I	■	E	T	T	E
P	R	Y	■	Y	U	A	N	■	D	A	C	E

ACROSS
1. Chances
5. Iridescent gem
9. Hold up
12. Verse
13. Glass panel
14. An age
15. Withered
16. Heroic
17. Play division
18. Indian currency
20. Greek goddesses of the seasons
22. Indian city
25. Marsh
26. Concur
27. Battle
28. Needlefish
31. Peruse
32. Prefix, not
33. At the bow of a vessel
34. Work unit
35. Sack
36. Infants
37. Domestic pet
38. Extravagant
39. Church council
42. The villain in Othello
43. New Zealand parrot
44. Is not
46. Marsh plant
50. Otic organ
51. Positions
52. Suffix, diminutive
53. Snoop
54. Monetary unit of China
55. Fresh-water fish

DOWN
1. Operations (colloq)
2. Female deer
3. The (German)
4. Daubed
5. Unseals
6. Father
7. Black bird
8. Lustful male
9. Back
10. Killer whale
11. Restrain
19. Not
21. Not off
22. Female horse
23. Maturing agent
24. Haul
25. Avid admirer
27. Flu (Colloq)
28. Mongolian desert
29. Greek god of war
30. 20th letter of the Hebrew alphabet
32. Henpeck
33. Privileged
35. Corporal
36. Sack
37. Perform
38. Roman
39. Beehive
40. Long period of time
41. Never
42. Ancient Peruvian
45. Former coin of France
47. Greek letter
48. Etcetera
49. Scottish river

solution 80

L	A	U	D		B	E	E	T		N O B

(Crossword solution grid)

Row 1: LAUD · BEET · NOB
Row 2: AREA · REEL · EGO
Row 3: BEYS · ULNA · TEA
Row 4: · · YAMS · LASER
Row 5: DANUBE · BON · ·
Row 6: HOARY · LAC · SET
Row 7: ANTE · PEA · RARE
Row 8: LEO · TED · AERIE
Row 9: · · BAG · EDDIES
Row 10: CHEEP · CROC · ·
Row 11: OIL · ECHO · OAKS
Row 12: OVA · RAID · ANEW
Row 13: PEN · SYCE · TINY

ACROSS
1. Praise
5. Root vegetable
9. Jack in cribbage
12. Region
13. Spool
14. The self
15. Turkish governors
16. Arm bone
17. An infusion
18. Sweet potatoes
20. Light beam
22. Austrian river
25. French, good
26. Grey
27. Resinous deposit
28. Become firm
31. Poker stake
32. Legume
33. Uncommon
34. Zodiac sign
35. Spread out for drying
36. Eagle's nest
37. Sack
38. Whirlpools
39. Chirp
42. Crocodile (Colloq)
43. Lubricant
44. Reverberate
46. Large trees
50. Eggs
51. Incursion
52. Once again
53. Female swan
54. Stable attendant
55. Wee

DOWN
1. Laboratory
2. Land measure
3. U-turn (Colloq)
4. Carnivorous marsupial
5. Mist
6. Long fish
7. Even (poet.)
8. Aztec god of rain
9. Devices for fishing
10. Double curve
11. Hog
19. To endure
21. Prefix meaning without
22. Indian pulses
23. First class (1-3)
24. Western pact
25. Bleat
27. Captained
28. Hindu garment
29. A Great Lake
30. Golf mounds
32. Wooden pin
33. Historically, a British soldier
35. Becomes narrow
36. Fuss
37. To exist
38. Wear away
39. Fowl enclosure
40. Bee nest
41. Dash
42. Stylish
45. Coral island
47. Black bird
48. Knowledge
49. Two-up

solution 81

F	I	N	N		H	Y	L	A		S	P	A
A	L	E	E		O	M	E	N		L	A	V
R	E	T	E		O	I	N	K		A	C	E
			D	E	E	R		L	O	V	E	R
B	E	L	F	R	Y		D	E	N			
O	D	O	U	R		Y	E	S		F	E	N
R	E	A	L		R	E	E		F	O	R	E
E	N	D		D	O	R		F	O	U	N	T
			D	A	B		T	U	R	R	E	T
A	N	C	O	N		I	O	N	S			
S	O	U		I	N	S	T		E	C	R	U
E	S	T		S	A	L	E		T	H	A	N
A	Y	E		H	E	E	D		I	I	W	I

ACROSS
1. Helsinki citizen
5. Tree frog
9. Mineral spring
12. To the sheltered side
13. Portent
14. Lavatory (Colloq)
15. Network of nerves
16. Hog sound
17. Top card
18. Antlered beast
20. Inamorato
22. Bell tower
25. Lair
26. Smell
27. Affirmative response
28. Marsh
31. Genuine
32. Female ruff
33. At the bow of a vessel
34. Finish
35. Beetle
36. Fountain
37. Skilled
38. Small tower
39. The elbow
42. Charged particles
43. Former coin of France
44. Current month
46. Colour of unbleached linen
50. Superlative suffix
51. Bargain event
52. Word used in comparisons
53. Affirmative vote
54. Obey
55. Hawaiian honeycreeper

DOWN
1. Distant
2. Island (France)
3. Seine
4. Necessary
5. Bunk
6. Primordial giant in Norse myth
7. Pet form of Leonard
8. Leg joints
9. European race
10. Step
11. Vow
19. Go wrong
21. Not off
22. Drill
23. Paradise
24. A burden
25. Scottish river
27. Your (Colloq)
28. Tetrad
29. Sea eagle
30. After deductions
32. Hold up
33. Norse god
35. Of Denmark
36. Amusement
37. Perform
38. Carried
39. At sea
40. Inquisitive
41. Strangely attractive
42. Small island
45. Not
47. Greek letter
48. Uncooked
49. Prefix, one

solution 82

M	A	N	X		C	O	O	T		D	A	D
A	R	E	A		U	N	C	O		O	D	A
E	T	O	N		L	U	A	U		U	Z	I
		T	I	P	S		C	A	G	E	S	
T	E	P	H	R	A		O	H	M			
E	Y	R	I	E		B	O	Y		I	M	P
C	R	O	C		O	O	F		P	L	E	A
H	A	D		T	W	A		A	R	I	A	N
		B	A	N		A	V	I	A	T	E	
T	A	P	E	R		O	G	E	E			
O	N	E		Z	I	N	G		S	A	K	E
R	O	W		A	C	E	R		T	O	E	A
E	N	S		N	E	R	O		S	K	A	T

ACROSS
1. Tailless cat
5. Diving bird
9. Father
12. Region
13. Remarkable
14. Room within a harem
15. English college
16. Hawaiian feast
17. Israeli submachine gun
18. Hints
20. Bird prisons
22. Volcanic material
25. Electrical resistance unit
26. Eagle's nest
27. Lad
28. Little devil
31. Crocodile (Colloq)
32. Money (Slang)
33. Prayer
34. Possessed
35. Two
36. Person born under the sign of the Ram
37. Prohibit
38. Fly an aircraft
39. Become narrow
42. Double curve
43. Monad
44. Zest
46. Rice wine
50. Tier
51. The maple
52. New Guinea currency unit
53. Abstract being
54. Fiddling Roman emperor
55. Card game

DOWN
1. Actress, - West
2. Talent
3. Prefix, new
4. Having a yellowish color
5. Guilt
6. Responsibility
7. Wood sorrel
8. Controversial
9. Cricketer, - Walters
10. Hoe-shaped axe
11. Speaking platform
19. Anger
21. Part of the verb "to be"
22. Technical college (Colloq)
23. Jaguarundi
24. Jab
25. Money (Slang)
27. Large snake
28. Hip bones
29. Flesh
30. Glass panel
32. Possess
33. Clergymen
35. Man of superior strength
36. Greeting
37. To exist
38. Aggression (Colloq)
39. Ripped
40. Soon
41. Church benches
42. Unique thing
45. Freeze
47. Very good (1-2)
48. New Zealand parrot
49. Consume

solution 83

U	R	N	S	■	T	B	A	R	■	C	A	T
S	O	O	K	■	A	E	R	O	■	O	C	H
A	B	B	A	■	R	A	K	U	■	L	I	E
■	■	■	T	H	O	U	■	B	U	D	D	Y
R	U	B	I	E	S	■	A	L	P	■	■	■
A	G	E	N	T	■	A	G	E	■	C	U	T
F	L	A	G	■	F	R	O	■	P	O	L	E
F	Y	N	■	V	I	M	■	S	H	I	N	E
■	■	■	T	U	T	■	T	I	A	R	A	S
I	D	O	L	■	E	I	R	E	■	■	■	■
T	W	A	■	C	U	R	T	■	T	E	A	L
E	E	N	■	A	N	I	L	■	O	G	L	E
M	R	S	■	N	I	N	E	■	N	O	T	E

ACROSS
1. Vases
5. Type of automatic gear selector (1-3)
9. Feline
12. Cry-baby
13. Prefix, air
14. Scottish expression
15. Swedish pop-group of the '70s
16. Rough earthenware
17. Falsehood
18. Old form or you or your
20. Chum
22. Ged gems
25. Peak
26. Spy
27. Mature
28. Sever
31. Pennant
32. To and -
33. Mast
34. Island of Denmark
35. Pep
36. Gleam
37. Minor admonishment
38. Coronets
39. Iodine solution
42. Ireland
43. Two
44. Terse
46. Freshwater duck
50. Even (poet.)
51. Indigo
52. Leer
53. Missus
54. Number of Muses
55. Musical symbol

DOWN
1. America (Abbr)
2. Hold up
3. Jack in cribbage
4. Performing on ice
5. Polynesian edible roots
6. Sweetheart
7. Noah's vessel
8. Russian money
9. Chill
10. Etching fluid
11. People in general
19. - up, excited
21. Toward the top
22. Rabble
23. Unattractive
24. A legume
25. In the past
27. Limb
28. Coconut husk fibre
29. Arm bone
30. Golf mounds
32. Spasm
33. Four-wheeled carriage
35. Roman god of fire
36. Knight's title
37. In the direction of
38. Name
39. A particular
40. One who is indebted
41. Levels of karate proficiency
42. Ireland
45. Prefix, one
47. The self
48. High-pitched
49. Sheltered side

solution 84

M	I	C	E		L	A	I	D		T	N	T
P	L	A	N		A	B	L	E		H	I	E
H	E	M	S		I	L	K	A		A	L	E
			N	A	R	Y		S	A	W	E	D
C	O	W	A	R	D		B	I	N			
A	P	O	R	T		O	I	L		S	E	A
K	A	L	E		D	A	B		M	O	R	N
E	L	D		S	U	R		P	A	U	S	E
		P	O	E		C	U	R	L	E	W	
S	N	A	I	L		A	L	S	O			
E	O	N		E	D	G	E		O	Y	E	Z
E	S	T		L	I	R	A		N	A	M	E
R	E	E		Y	E	A	N		S	H	U	N

ACROSS
1. Small rodents
5. Reposed
9. An explosive
12. Scheme
13. Capable
14. Hasten
15. Garment edges
16. Every
17. Beer
18. Never
20. Cut wood
22. Craven person
25. Garbage can
26. Nautical, to the left
27. Lubricant
28. Large body of water
31. Cabbagelike plant
32. Skilled
33. Morning
34. Antiquity
35. Prefix, over
36. Brief halt
37. "The Raven" author
38. Whimbrel
39. Garden pest
42. As well as
43. An age
44. Brink
46. Town crier's call
50. Superlative suffix
51. Italian currency
52. Title
53. Female ruff
54. Lamb
55. Avoid

DOWN
1. Miles per hour
2. Island (France)
3. Eccentric wheel
4. Entrap
5. Scottish lord
6. Skilfully
7. Family
8. Clockwise
9. Melt
10. African river
11. - off, began golf game
19. Talent
21. Prefix meaning without
22. Shaped mass of food
23. Iridescent gem
24. A plain
25. Infant's protective garment
27. Paddle
28. Inner spirit
29. Gaelic
30. Once again
32. Owing
33. Leaves stranded
35. Exclusively
36. Purulence
37. The ratio between circumference and diameter
38. Wash
39. Prophet
40. Proboscis
41. Poker stake
42. Taj Mahal site
45. Expire
47. Exclamation of disgust
48. Australian bird
49. Buddhist sect

solution 85

M	E	E	T	■	W	A	S	H	■	S	E	E
I	R	E	S	■	H	I	K	E	■	L	A	G
R	A	L	E	■	A	D	I	T	■	O	V	A
■	■	■	T	A	R	S	■	E	M	B	E	D
A	U	S	S	I	E	■	O	R	E	■	■	■
O	P	T	E	D	■	M	O	O	■	Y	O	B
N	O	U	S	■	O	A	F	■	C	O	X	A
E	N	D	■	A	I	R	■	R	A	G	E	S
■	■	■	A	W	L	■	I	O	D	I	N	E
A	B	A	S	H	■	I	N	C	A	■	■	■
W	O	G	■	I	O	N	S	■	V	E	T	O
A	R	E	■	L	A	K	E	■	E	L	A	N
Y	E	R	■	E	R	S	T	■	R	I	D	E

ACROSS
1. Greet
5. Cleanse
9. Witness
12. Angers
13. Long walk
14. A delay
15. Death rattle
16. Entrance
17. Eggs
18. Sailors
20. Solidly fix in surrounding mass
22. An Australian
25. Crude mineral
26. Chose
27. Cattle low
28. Teenage lout
31. Commonsense
32. Clumsy person
33. Hip
34. Finish
35. Atmosphere
36. Storms
37. Shoemaker's tool
38. Violet antiseptic
39. Make ashamed
42. Ancient Peruvian
43. Flu (Colloq)
44. Charged particles
46. Override
50. Land measure
51. Tarn
52. Dash
53. Your (Colloq)
54. Former
55. Travel on

DOWN
1. Russian community
2. An age
3. Conger
4. Sleeping sickness flies
5. Maori hut
6. Helps
7. Snow runner
8. Heterosexual (Colloq)
9. Untidy person
10. Roof overhang
11. Minor oath
19. Assist
21. Objective case of I
22. First class (1-3)
23. On top of
24. Breeding horse
25. Money (Slang)
27. Spoil
28. Practitioner of yoga
29. Beasts of burden
30. Bottom
32. Lubricant
33. Corpse
35. For a short time
36. Fabulous bird
37. Similar to
38. Piece put in
39. Absent
40. Drill
41. Maturing agent
42. Writing fluids
45. Paddle
47. Biblical high priest
48. Small amount
49. Monad

solution 86

C	R	A	M		K	A	K	A		H	I	S
A	U	R	A		A	B	E	L		A	L	E
B	E	T	H		U	L	N	A		Z	I	T
			J	U	R	Y		R	H	E	A	S
O	C	T	O	P	I		S	U	E			
G	L	E	N	S		Q	O	M		M	R	S
R	A	N	G		C	U	B		S	O	I	L
E	M	S		B	A	A		D	U	O	M	O
			H	E	W		S	U	B	D	E	B
P	L	A	I	D		S	T	O	T			
A	I	L		E	S	K	Y		E	N	O	W
L	A	P		W	A	I	L		E	A	V	E
E	R	S		S	O	M	E		N	E	A	T

ACROSS
1. Pack fully
5. New Zealand parrot
9. Belonging to him
12. Subtle emanation
13. Cain's victim
14. Beer
15. 2nd letter of the Hebrew alphabet
16. Arm bone
17. Acne pimple
18. Panel
20. Ostrich-like birds
22. Eight tentacled creatures
25. Take to court
26. Valleys
27. City in NW Iran
28. Missus
31. Phoned
32. Young bear
33. Dirt
34. Printer's measures
35. Bleat
36. Cathedral
37. Chop
38. Subdebutante
39. Tartan
42. Springing gait
43. Sicken
44. Portable ice-box
46. Enough
50. Fold
51. Ululate
52. Roof overhang
53. Bitter vetch
54. A few
55. Tidy

DOWN
1. Taxi
2. Regret
3. Talent
4. Chinese game
5. New Zealand evergreen tree
6. Skilfully
7. Knowledge
8. Warning bell
9. Obscurity
10. Hip bones
11. Hardens
19. Raises
21. Masculine pronoun
22. Monster
23. Large mollusc
24. Decades
25. Weep
27. As
28. Atmosphere
29. Hoarfrost
30. Untidy person
32. Crow call
33. Person approaching the teens
35. Covers with dew
36. Twosome
37. Hello there
38. Manner
39. Wan
40. Fibber
41. Peaks
42. Glide on surface
45. Cracker biscuit
47. Not
48. Eggs
49. Soak

solution 87

W	A	I	L		T	S	A	R		M	P	H
O	I	L	Y		E	L	L	E		A	L	E
O	M	E	N		R	A	L	E		L	A	M
			C	A	M	P		K	N	I	T	S
C	A	P	E	R	S		G	E	O			
E	X	E	A	T		B	A	D		B	Y	E
L	I	N	N		Y	A	G		N	A	I	L
L	S	D		B	A	N		J	E	R	K	S
			G	O	O		B	A	W	B	E	E
B	R	O	O	D		A	E	R	Y			
O	U	R		I	D	E	A		O	P	E	N
A	B	Y		L	O	O	T		R	A	G	A
S	E	X		Y	E	N	S		K	N	O	B

ACROSS
1. Ululate
5. Russian emperor
9. Miles per hour
12. Greasy
13. Australian super-model
14. Beer
15. Portent
16. Death rattle
17. Thrash
18. Temporary settlement
20. Weaves wool
22. Antics
25. Prefix, the earth
26. Leave of absence
27. Evil
28. Farewell
31. Waterfall
32. Synthetic yttrium aluminum garnet
33. Metal spike
34. Hallucinogenic drug
35. Prohibit
36. Tugs
37. Sticky stuff
38. Old Scottish bullion coin
39. Nide
42. Ethereal
43. Of us
44. Notion
46. Candid
50. To endure
51. Booty
52. Hindu music
53. Gender
54. Desires
55. Door handle

DOWN
1. Court
2. Intention
3. Island (France)
4. Sharp-sighted
5. Expressions
6. Hit with hand
7. Everything
8. Smelled foul
9. Republic in W Africa
10. Plot of ground
11. Garment edges
19. Talent
21. Negative vote
22. Prison room
23. Line of revolution
24. Hang
25. To silence
27. Prohibit
28. Point of hook
29. Argument
30. Otherwise
32. Legendary emperor of China
33. The *Big Apple* (3,4)
35. Corporal
36. Jolt
37. Depart
38. Vanquishes
39. Large snakes
40. Hick
41. Large African antelope
42. Great age
45. Female deer
47. Kitchen utensil
48. The self
49. Arrest

solution 88

S	N	I	P		G	N	A	R		Z	A	P
L	A	N	E		I	O	T	A		E	V	E
Y	E	N	S		S	T	E	T		B	E	E
			T	I	M	E		I	N	U	R	N
B	O	L	E	R	O		O	N	O			
A	D	O	R	E		B	I	G		A	C	E
B	E	N	S		S	O	L		C	L	A	N
A	R	E		K	O	A		P	R	O	U	D
			T	U	N		W	H	E	E	L	S
M	E	D	O	C		A	R	I	A			
E	Y	E		H	I	V	E		S	H	I	V
A	R	C		E	V	E	N		E	A	S	E
T	E	A		N	E	S	S		D	O	M	E

ACROSS
1. Pare
5. Growl
9. Annihilate
12. Narrow country road
13. Jot
14. First woman
15. Desires
16. Printer's mark, keep
17. Hive insect
18. Hour
20. Inter ashes
22. Short jacket
25. Yoko -
26. Worship
27. Large
28. Top card
31. Scottish hills
32. The sun
33. Tribe
34. Land measure
35. Hawaiian acacia
36. Haughty
37. Large barrel
38. Trundles
39. French claret
42. Opera solo
43. Optic organ
44. Bee nest
46. Switchblade
50. Part of a circle
51. Level
52. Relax
53. An infusion
54. Scottish headland
55. Cupola

DOWN
1. Wily
2. Not
3. Tavern
4. Harasses
5. Gadget
6. Musical symbol
7. Dined
8. Unranked seaman
9. Indian ox
10. Vow
11. Hammer head
19. Anger
21. Negative vote
22. Small yeast cake
23. River in central Europe
24. Solitary
25. Lubricant
27. Large snake
28. Agave
29. Hood-like membrane
30. Finishes
32. Male offspring
33. Wrinkled
35. Yeast-raised coffeecake
36. Greek letter
37. In the direction of
38. Songbirds
39. Flesh
40. Australian explorer
41. Prefix, ten
42. Birds
45. I have
47. Monetary unit of Vietnam
48. Doctrine
49. Victory sign

solution 89

C	R	U	X		I	B	I	S		L	E	A
H	O	N	E		L	I	F	T		I	L	L
E	M	I	R		I	N	F	O		D	U	E
			O	R	A	D		D	H	O	L	E
S	O	U	S	E	D		A	G	E			
L	U	R	I	D		C	U	E		S	E	N
O	R	T	S		A	U	K		E	A	V	E
P	S	I		C	A	B		E	A	G	E	R
			A	A	H		S	T	R	A	N	D
C	H	A	S	M		O	U	C	H			
O	I	L		B	O	L	D		A	R	C	H
I	D	O		E	N	D	S		R	H	E	A
F	E	E		R	O	S	Y		T	O	T	O

ACROSS
1. A cross
5. Sacred Egyptian bird
9. Meadow
12. Sharpen
13. Raise
14. Sick
15. Islamic chieftain
16. Information
17. Owing
18. Toward the mouth
20. Wild Asian dog
22. Pickled
25. Mature
26. Ghastly
27. Prompt
28. Monetary unit of Japan
31. Food scraps
32. Diving bird
33. Roof overhang
34. Pressure symbol
35. Taxi
36. Keen
37. Exclamation of surprise
38. Leave high and dry
39. Rift
42. Ornamental brooch
43. Lubricant
44. Daring
46. Curved entrance
50. Revised form of Esperanto
51. Finishes
52. Ostrich-like bird
53. A charge
54. Blushing
55. In -, in all

DOWN
1. - Guevara
2. Gipsy lad
3. Prefix, one
4. Abnormal dryness of the skin
5. Homer's epic
6. Tie
7. If and only if
8. Gorge
9. Public swimming pool
10. 12th month of the Jewish calendar
11. To the sheltered side
19. Colour
21. Masculine pronoun
22. Splash
23. Yours and mine
24. Upper respiratory tract infection
25. Diving bird
27. Young bear
28. Heroic story
29. Level
30. Dweeb
32. Exclamation of surprise
33. US aviatrix, Amelia -
35. Slight arch
36. Etcetera
37. Similar to
38. Resembling suds
39. Skullcap
40. Conceal
41. Agave
42. One's parents (Colloq)
45. Yoko -
47. 17th letter of the Greek alphabet
48. Prefix, whale
49. Monetary unit of Vietnam

solution 90

P	E	A	R		C	E	L	T		S	E	W
A	E	R	O		O	B	O	E		E	T	A
P	L	E	A		A	B	B	A		R	U	N
			C	A	T	S		C	U	B	I	T
V	A	S	H	T	I		P	U	P			
E	M	C	E	E		L	I	P		R	A	J
S	E	A	S		D	O	E		E	U	R	O
T	N	T		H	A	G		N	A	N	C	E
		D	A	B		M	A	R	S	H	Y	
I	O	D	O	L		D	I	N	S			
S	H	Y		L	A	Y	S		H	A	N	G
L	I	E		E	G	A	D		O	B	I	E
E	O	S		Y	O	K	O		T	Y	P	E

ACROSS
1. Pome
5. Gael
9. Stitch
12. Prefix, air
13. Hautboy
14. Greek letter
15. Prayer
16. Swedish pop-group of the '70s
17. Flee
18. Felines
20. Biblical measure
22. Queen of Ahasuerus
25. Young dog
26. Master of ceremonies
27. Mouth part
28. British rule in India
31. Oceans
32. Female deer
33. Wallaroo
34. An explosive
35. Beldam
36. Effeminate male
37. Skilled
38. Like a marsh
39. Iodine solution
42. Rackets
43. Timid
44. Puts down
46. Drape
50. Falsehood
51. Minor oath
52. Off-Broadway theater award
53. Greek goddess of the dawn
54. - Ono
55. Variety

DOWN
1. Nipple
2. Conger
3. Land measure
4. Cockroaches (Colloq)
5. Raccoonlike carnivore
6. Wanes
7. Throw lightly
8. Item in a tea service
9. Yugoslavian
10. Sewing case
11. Desire
19. Dined
21. Toward the top
22. Waistcoat
23. Prayer ending
24. Shoo
25. Pastry item
27. Large tree remnant
28. Cricket scores
29. Curved entrance
30. Young kangaroo
32. Skilled
33. Range of hearing
35. English astronomer
36. Grandmother
37. Perform
38. Botch
39. Small island
40. U.S. State
41. Stains
42. Aborigine of Borneo
45. In the past
47. To endure
48. Pinch
49. Horse command

solution 91

D	A	F	T		Q	U	I	D		S	B	S
E	R	I	E		U	R	D	U		L	E	I
R	E	N	D		A	E	O	N		U	L	T
		I	L	K	A		C	A	R	T	E
J	O	C	O	S	E		T	E	N		
A	L	O	U	D		T	I	S		Y	O	N
T	I	E	S		B	A	T		C	O	D	A
O	D	D		G	O	B		Y	U	K	O	N
	I	D	A		C	A	M	E	R	A	
J	A	F	F	A		L	A	M	S		
I	D	E		N	E	O	N		H	E	W	N
V	A	S		S	K	A	T		A	L	E	E
E	M	S		K	E	N	O		W	I	D	E

ACROSS
1. Foolish
5. One pound sterling
9. Ethnic telecaster
12. A Great Lake
13. Official language of Pakistan
14. Garland
15. Tear
16. Great age
17. Last month
18. Every
20. Menu
22. Playful
25. Decade
26. Audibly
27. It is
28. Over there
31. Binds
32. Flying mammal
33. Musical ending
34. Rum
35. Sailor
36. Canadian province
37. Highest mountain in Crete
38. Photography requisite
39. Israeli orange
42. Thrashes
43. Carp-like fish
44. Lighting gas
46. Chopped
50. Vessel or duct
51. Card game
52. To the sheltered side
53. Printer's measures
54. Lotto-like gambling game
55. Broad

DOWN
1. The (German)
2. Land measure
3. Fish part
4. Monotonous
5. Tremble
6. Fertiliser
7. Revised form of Esperanto
8. Boneheads
9. Elide
10. Leather strap
11. Situate
19. Hallucinogenic drug
21. Prefix meaning without
22. Jet-assisted takeoff
23. Fetid
24. Student at mixed school
25. Small bird
27. Label
28. Pair of oxen
29. Scent
30. Grandmother
32. Large snake
33. Gratuity
35. Danzig
36. Sweet potato
37. Providing
38. Division of a long poem
39. Jitterbug
40. First man
41. Heraldry, wide horizontal stripe on shield
42. Advance money
45. Supplement existence
47. Biblical high priest
48. Marry
49. Born

solution 92

A	L	A	R	■	C	R	E	W	V	U	G
W	E	R	E	■	H	A	V	E	I	S	A
E	A	T	S	■	A	G	E	D	V	E	E
■	■	T	U	F	A	■	G	N	A	R	L
D	E	M	O	T	E	■	G	E	O	■	■
A	P	A	C	E	■	M	A	D	■	S	O	P
C	O	R	K	■	G	A	G	■	E	T	N	A
E	S	T	■	B	U	S	■	G	A	Y	E	R
■	■	S	U	M	■	M	E	R	E	S	T
L	A	B	O	R	■	K	E	L	P	■	■
E	R	A	■	D	E	E	M	■	L	A	W	S
E	A	R	■	E	R	G	O	■	U	T	A	H
S	B	S	■	N	E	S	S	■	G	E	N	E

ACROSS
1. Having wings
5. Ship's company
9. Small cavity in a rock
12. Once existed
13. Possess
14. Mount - , N.W. Qld. mining town
15. Food
16. Old
17. Victory sign
18. Porous limestone
20. Knot
22. Lower in rank
25. Prefix, the earth
26. Abreast
27. Insane
28. Saturate
31. Stopper
32. To silence
33. Sicilian volcano
34. Superlative suffix
35. Public transport
36. Merrier
37. Total
38. Smallest
39. Australian political party
42. Large seaweed
43. An age
44. Consider
46. Statutes
50. Otic organ
51. Therefore
52. American state
53. Ethnic telecaster
54. Scottish headland
55. Hereditary factor

DOWN
1. Reverential fear
2. Meadow
3. Talent
4. Replenish
5. Abrade
6. Hindu music
7. First woman
8. Having the shape of a wedge
9. Exclamation of acclaim
10. Consumer
11. Erse
19. Small truck
21. Negative vote
22. Fresh-water fish
23. Epic poetry
24. Shopping centre
25. To silence
27. Mothers
28. Eye inflammation
29. Single items
30. Separate
32. Common eucalypt
33. Plug to keep out noise
35. Heavy load
36. Congeal
37. Therefore
38. Brief notes
39. Dregs
40. Semite
41. Prohibits
42. Beer barrels
45. Before
47. Dined
48. Ashen
49. That woman

solution 93

D	I	N	G	■	L	W	E	I	■	F	O	E
A	R	E	A	■	A	E	O	N	■	L	S	D
L	E	E	R	■	N	E	S	S	■	I	L	E
■	■	■	B	E	C	K	■	A	N	C	O	N
D	O	N	A	T	E	■	O	N	O	■	■	■
O	M	E	G	A	■	L	A	E	■	D	E	E
D	A	R	E	■	O	O	F	■	S	H	A	Y
O	R	D	■	F	A	X	■	C	H	A	S	E
■	■	■	O	A	K	■	F	O	I	L	E	D
S	T	A	R	R	■	R	A	S	H	■	■	■
H	I	D	■	M	O	A	T	■	T	Y	P	E
U	N	I	■	E	D	N	A	■	Z	E	A	L
N	E	T	■	R	A	I	L	■	U	R	T	I

ACROSS
1. Cause to ring by striking
5. Monetary unit of Angola
9. Enemy
12. Region
13. Great age
14. Hallucinogenic drug
15. Ogle
16. Scottish headland
17. Island (France)
18. Summon
20. The elbow
22. Give to
25. Yoko -
26. Greek letter
27. New Guinea seaport
28. Scottish river
31. Challenge
32. Money (Slang)
33. Chaise
34. W.A. river
35. Machine for sending documents
36. Pursue
37. Large tree
38. Thwarted
39. Beatles' drummer, Ringo -
42. Hasty
43. Concealed
44. Water filled barricade
46. Variety
50. Prefix, one
51. Dame - Everage, Humphries' character
52. Enthusiasm
53. Seine
54. Train track
55. Upper respiratory tract infection

DOWN
1. Indian dish
2. Anger
3. Born
4. Trash
5. Cavalry spear
6. Seven days
7. Greek goddess of the dawn
8. Demented
9. French policeman
10. Capital of Norway
11. Paradise
19. Greek letter
21. Negative vote
22. Extinct bird
23. - Khayyam
24. Dweeb
25. Clumsy person
27. Brine-cured salmon
28. Indian pulses
29. Relax
30. Looked over
32. Large tree
33. Tibetan breed of small dog
35. Person who operates a farm
36. Long-leaved lettuce
37. Otherwise
38. Deadly
39. Avoid
40. Prong
41. Entrance
42. Indian queen
45. Room within a harem
47. Your (Colloq)
48. Dab
49. Biblical high priest

solution 94

J	U	D	Y		S	T	O	A		B	O	D
U	N	I	T		C	A	R	S		E	A	R
T	I	N	T		E	N	D	S		A	H	A
			R	I	N	G		O	A	K	U	M
A	L	P	I	N	E		M	R	S			
R	E	R	U	N		D	O	T		A	M	U
T	E	A	M		G	A	M		C	Z	A	R
S	K	Y		M	E	M		F	L	A	G	S
			D	Y	E		U	R	A	N	I	A
T	A	B	O	O		S	N	O	B			
O	H	O		P	O	T	S		B	O	O	M
F	O	R		I	L	I	A		E	C	H	O
F	Y	N		A	E	R	Y		R	A	M	P

ACROSS
1. Wife of Punch
5. Portico
9. A person
12. Military detachment
13. Vehicles
14. Otic organ
15. Hue
16. Finishes
17. Exclamation of surprise
18. Encircle
20. Loose fiber used for caulking
22. Pertaining to the Alps
25. Missus
26. Television repeat
27. Speck
28. Atomic mass unit
31. Side
32. Leg
33. Emperor of Russia
34. Firmament
35. 13th letter of the Hebrew alphabet
36. Pennants
37. Change colour of
38. The Muse of astronomy
39. Forbidden
42. Scorning person
43. Exclamation of surprise
44. Cooking implements
46. Time of prosperity
50. In favour of
51. Hip bones
52. Reverberate
53. Island of Denmark
54. Ethereal
55. Sloping walkway

DOWN
1. Protrude
2. Prefix, one
3. Racket
4. Rare metallic element
5. Vista
6. Sharp taste
7. W.A. river
8. Classify
9. Bill
10. Island of Hawaii
11. Small drink of liquor
19. Tavern
21. Similar to
22. Non-scientific studies
23. Welsh emblem
24. Make supplication
25. Mother (US)
27. Weir
28. Islamic call to prayer
29. The three wise men
30. Bear constellation
32. Horse command
33. Curdled milk
35. Nearsightedness
36. To and -
37. Perform
38. Retract
39. Dandy
40. Nautical call
41. Nee
42. Agitate
45. Bullfight call
47. Wood sorrel
48. Electrical resistance unit
49. Swab

solution 95

Z	E	B	U		R	E	T	E		H	A	N
A	E	O	N		E	A	R	N		A	C	E
P	L	O	T		A	V	I	D		T	N	T
			R	A	T	E		U	P	S	E	T
C	A	N	U	T	E		L	E	I			
A	B	A	T	E		W	A	S		W	H	O
G	U	S	H		P	I	G		C	A	I	N
E	T	A		L	O	G		B	U	R	K	E
			D	U	X		E	A	R	N	E	R
G	A	B	O	N		A	J	A	R			
O	L	E		G	A	M	E		A	U	T	O
D	E	E		E	X	E	C		N	E	A	P
S	E	N		S	E	N	T		T	Y	P	E

ACROSS
1. Indian ox
5. Network of nerves
9. A dynasty in China
12. Great age
13. Merit
14. Top card
15. Plan
16. Eager
17. An explosive
18. Assess
20. Make unhappy
22. King who couldn't hold back the tide
25. Garland
26. Wane
27. Once existed
28. Which person
31. Spurt forth
32. Hog
33. First son of Adam and Eve
34. Greek letter
35. Large tree remnant
36. Murder by suffocation
37. Top pupil
38. Breadwinner
39. Republic in W equatorial Africa
42. Slightly open
43. Bullfight call
44. Brave
46. Motor car
50. Scottish river
51. Executive Officer
52. Lowest high tide
53. Monetary unit of Japan
54. Dispatched
55. Variety

DOWN
1. Annihilate
2. Conger
3. Jeer
4. Lie
5. Consumed again
6. Roof overhang
7. Prefix, three
8. Invests
9. Headwear
10. Adolescent pimples
11. After deductions
19. Dined
21. The ratio between circumference and diameter
22. Bird prison
23. Adjoin
24. U.S. space agency
25. A delay
27. Hairpiece
28. Caution
29. Long walk
30. Unique thing
32. Plague
33. Seedless raisin
35. Thrusts forward
36. Bleat
37. Perform
38. Oust
39. Deities
40. To the sheltered side
41. "Has - ". Person who once was
42. Prayer ending
45. Chop
47. U-turn (Colloq)
48. Faucet
49. Open

solution 96

H	E	A	P		O	R	A	D		C	U	R
O	R	C	A		C	O	V	E		A	R	E
Y	E	T	I		E	P	E	E		L	S	D
		S	H	A	Y		M	A	M	A	S	
G	A	W	A	I	N		J	E	T			
L	O	I	N	S		W	A	D		C	A	P
U	N	D	O		C	A	M		E	R	G	O
T	E	E		Y	I	N		C	A	I	R	O
			S	O	D		H	E	R	B	A	L
B	E	F	O	G		O	O	P	S			
E	A	R		U	P	D	O		H	O	B	O
E	R	A		R	Y	O	T		O	N	E	R
S	L	Y		T	A	R	S		T	O	E	D

ACROSS
1. Pile
5. Toward the mouth
9. Worthless dog
12. Killer whale
13. Bay
14. Land measure
15. Abominable snowman
16. Fencing sword
17. Hallucinogenic drug
18. Chaise
20. Mothers
22. Nephew of King Arthur
25. Black
26. Hips
27. Bundle of money
28. Item of headwear
31. Unwrap
32. Eccentric wheel
33. Therefore
34. Golf peg
35. - and Yang
36. Egyptian capital
37. Soil
38. Consisting of herbs
39. Hake hazy
42. Expression used when accident happens
43. Otic organ
44. Upswept hairdo
46. Tramp
50. An age
51. Indian peasant
52. Unique thing
53. Wily
54. Sailors
55. Having pedal digits

DOWN
1. Bingo-like game
2. Before
3. Play division
4. Countryman
5. Large body of water
6. Resembling a rope
7. Greeting
8. Thought
9. Serene
10. Bear constellation
11. Clarets
19. Belonging to him
21. Near to
22. Surfeit
23. First class (1-3)
24. Broad
25. Fruit conserve
27. Ashen
28. Manger
29. Taj Mahal site
30. Pond
32. Spanish hero
33. Range of hearing
35. Curdled milk
36. Brown-capped boletus mushroom
37. Therefore
38. Loud derisory cries
39. Hive insects
40. Nobleman
41. Ravel
42. Scent
45. Monetary unit of Burma
47. Yoko -
48. Hive insect
49. W.A. river

solution 97

```
P I E S  █  L A I D  █  V A N
E C R U  █  E D D O  █  I V E
W E N D  █  V E S T  █  N O N
█  █  A M E N  █  I N A N E
R E G N A L  █  O N O  █  █
A C R I D  █  W I G  █  S O B
C H I C  █  S O L  █  F I N E
E O N  █  D U E  █  B O N E D
█  █  I R E  █  E U C H R E
Q U A S I  █  T A N S  █  █
U P S  █  E D I T  █  L O S E
I D A  █  S A K E  █  E P E E
T O P  █  T W I N  █  S E W N
```

ACROSS
1. Pastry items
5. Reposed
9. Forefront
12. Colour of unbleached linen
13. Root of the taro
14. I have
15. Direct one's way
16. Waistcoat
17. Prefix, not
18. Prayer ending
20. Vapid
22. Pertaining to reign
25. Yoko -
26. Bitter
27. Hairpiece
28. Weep
31. Stylish
32. The sun
33. Amerce
34. An age
35. Owing
36. Filleted
37. Anger
38. Card game
39. Virtual
42. Converts to leather
43. Raises
44. Redact
46. Be defeated
50. Highest mountain in Crete
51. Rice wine
52. Fencing sword
53. Apex
54. One of two identical people
55. Stitched

DOWN
1. Church bench
2. Freeze
3. Sea eagle
4. Pertaining to the Sudan
5. Even
6. Capital of Yemen
7. Egos
8. Being foolishly fond of
9. Musical instrument of India
10. Shakespeare's river
11. Hawaiian goose
19. Insane
21. Negative vote
22. Sprint contest
23. Reverberate
24. Smile
25. Lubricant
27. Alas
28. Hyperbolic sine
29. Unique thing
30. English monk
32. Take to court
33. Sailors' forward cabins
35. Most parched
36. Bread roll
37. Part of the verb to be
38. Consumed
39. Stop
40. Upswept hairdo
41. As soon as possible
42. Maori image
45. Black bird
47. Open
48. Stitch
49. Even (poet.)

solution 98

M	A	I	L		J	A	C	K		H	A	M
A	L	O	E		U	S	E	R		O	L	E
X	E	N	O		D	A	T	A		R	E	E
			N	E	A	P		K	N	A	C	K
J	E	W	I	S	H		G	E	O			
A	G	E	N	T		B	O	N		Y	E	R
R	O	L	E		B	I	O		J	I	V	E
L	S	D		S	A	N		M	O	P	E	D
		P	E	A		C	O	H	E	R	E	
N	O	R	I	A		G	O	O	N			
A	G	E		M	A	A	M		D	U	N	E
I	L	E		E	P	E	E		O	P	A	L
L	E	D		N	E	A	R		E	S	P	Y

ACROSS
1. Chain armour
5. Knave
9. Overact
12. Agave
13. Consumer
14. Bullfight call
15. Prefix, foreign
16. Information
17. Female ruff
18. Lowest high tide
20. Skill
22. Pertaining to Jews
25. Prefix, the earth
26. Spy
27. French, good
28. Your (Colloq)
31. Part played
32. Prefix, life
33. Jitterbug
34. Hallucinogenic drug
35. Japanese word of respect
36. Sulked
37. Legume
38. Stick together
39. Water wheel
42. Hired thug
43. Mature
44. Madam
46. Sand hill
50. Island (France)
51. Fencing sword
52. Iridescent gem
53. Captained
54. Close to
55. Glimpse

DOWN
1. Maximum
2. Beer
3. Charged particle
4. Lionlike
5. One of the 12 tribes of Israel
6. As soon as possible
7. Prefix, whale
8. Mythical sea monster
9. Israeli round dance
10. Smart - , show-off
11. Humble
19. Superlative suffix
21. Negative vote
22. Medieval Scandinavian chieftain
23. Personalities
24. Fuse together
25. Sticky stuff
27. Garbage can
28. Exclamation of fright
29. Always
30. Advise
32. Bleat
33. Average man
35. Sailors
36. Cattle low
37. The ratio between circumference and diameter
38. Arriver
39. Metal spike
40. Leer
41. Marsh plant
42. Greek goddess of the earth
45. Primate
47. Raises
48. Doze
49. Cathedral city

solution 99

E	V	E	R		D	U	A	D		U	H	F
S	E	M	I		E	R	S	E		R	A	Y
P	E	S	O		A	A	H	S		E	L	K
			T	A	L	L		C	H	A	F	E
B	A	S	E	S	T		E	R	E			
U	S	U	R	P		S	T	Y		D	O	B
Y	E	N	S		L	E	A		T	U	N	E
S	A	N		K	E	A		O	A	R	E	D
			G	E	O		A	R	B	O	R	S
D	E	C	O	Y		U	N	C	O			
A	W	E		P	O	R	N		R	E	N	D
Z	E	N		A	L	S	O		E	P	E	E
E	S	T		D	D	A	Y		T	I	D	E

ACROSS
1. Always
5. Couple
9. Television frequency
12. Prefix, part
13. Gaelic
14. Sunbeam
15. Mexican currency
16. Exclamations of surprise
17. Moose
18. Lofty
20. Abrade
22. Most mean
25. Before
26. Seize illegally
27. Pig enclosure
28. Tell on
31. Desires
32. Meadow
33. Melody
34. Japanese word of respect
35. New Zealand parrot
36. Rowed
37. Prefix, the earth
38. Bowers
39. Lure
42. Remarkable
43. Reverential fear
44. Pornography (Colloq)
46. Tear
50. Buddhist sect
51. As well as
52. Fencing sword
53. Superlative suffix
54. June 6, 1944
55. Ocean fluctuation

DOWN
1. Extrasensory perception
2. Victory sign
3. Printer's measures
4. People in rebellion
5. Distributed cards
6. European mountain range
7. Fire remains
8. Discover
9. Fertiliser
10. One of two equal parts
11. Bag-shaped fish trap
19. Egyptian serpent
21. Masculine pronoun
22. Purchases
23. At sea
24. E Indian shrub yielding hemp
25. Greek letter
27. Large body of water
28. Former coin of Spain
29. Unique thing
30. Cots
32. Zodiac sign
33. Stool
35. Panel of special keys
36. Killer whale
37. Depart
38. Bother
39. Stupefy
40. Female sheep
41. Monetary unit
42. Bear constellation
45. Aged
47. Prefix, over
48. - Kelly
49. Scottish river

solution 100

W	A	N	D		T	B	A	R		C	E	T
A	G	U	E		I	L	I	A		O	L	E
X	E	N	O		N	A	R	C		M	A	E
			R	A	G	E		K	H	A	N	S
R	O	U	B	L	E		F	E	E			
A	D	L	I	B		G	E	T		F	B	I
P	E	N	T		B	E	D		K	E	E	N
E	R	A		G	O	O		F	L	U	N	K
		W	A	X		G	L	A	D	E	S	
D	W	E	E	B		B	R	U	T			
E	A	R		B	I	R	O		S	I	G	N
E	G	O		L	A	I	D		C	R	E	E
M	E	S		E	M	M	Y		H	E	E	D

ACROSS
1. Baton
5. Type of automatic gear selector (1-3)
9. Prefix, whale
12. Fever
13. Hip bones
14. Bullfight call
15. Prefix, foreign
16. Narcotics agent
17. Actress, - West
18. Storm
20. Persian lords
22. Russian money
25. A charge
26. Improvise (speech)
27. Obtain
28. Law enforcement agency
31. Confined
32. Cot
33. Avid
34. An age
35. Sticky stuff
36. Fail
37. Bee product
38. Valleys
39. Nerd
42. Very dry champagne
43. Otic organ
44. Pen
46. Portent
50. The self
51. Reposed
52. American Indian
53. My, French (Plural)
54. U.S. TV award
55. Obey

DOWN
1. Bee product
2. Mature
3. Cloistered woman
4. Leave orbit
5. Tint
6. Blue-gray
7. Atmosphere
8. Din
9. Unconsciousness
10. Dash
11. Golf mounds
19. Long-sleeved linen vestment
21. Masculine pronoun
22. Take by force
23. River in central Europe
24. Arm bone
25. Gave food to
27. Prefix, the earth
28. Ongoing hostility
29. Prefix, well
30. Writing fluids
32. Crate
33. Casual gathering
35. Jabber
36. Influenza
37. Plural of I
38. Sleazy
39. Consider
40. Money paid for work
41. Greek god of love
42. Projecting edge
45. Braggart (Colloq) (1.2)
47. Anger
48. Horse command
49. - Kelly

Manufactured by Amazon.ca
Bolton, ON